GLASS ANIMALS

GLASS ANIMALS

3,500 YEARS OF ARTISTRY AND DESIGN

BY ALBANE DOLEZ

HARRY N. ABRAMS, INC., PUBLISHERS, NEW YORK

Project Director: Robert Morton
Editor: Ruth A. Peltason
Designer: Ana Rogers

Picture Research: Pamela Bass, Frederic Roy
Portions of this manuscript translated by Richard Miller

Editorial Note: Objects in this book are not reproduced actual size. All dimensions are given in centimeters. One inch equals 2.54 centimeters.

Library of Congress Cataloging-in-Publication Data

Dolez, Albane.
    Glass animals: 3,500 years of artistry/by Albane Dolez.
        p.   cm.
    Includes index.
    ISBN 0-8109-1034-9
    1. Glass animals—History.   I. Title.
NK5440.A55D65   1988
748.8—dc19   88-968
                                                        CIP

TITLE PAGE: Peter Aldridge and Jane Osborn-Smith for Steuben Glass. *Swan Bowl.* 1985. Blown crystal. Diameter 22.9 cm, height 20.3 cm. Steuben Glass, New York

CONTENTS

INTRODUCTION

I have long been fascinated by glass—with its contrasting properties of transparency, fragility, and solidity—and having worked professionally with glass for several years, my passion for it has remained strong. Pursuing that interest, I wrote numerous magazine articles on such glass manufacturers as Steuben and Daum, and on the superior Corning Museum of Glass in upstate New York. Studying that collection gave me the idea for this book.

My research began some five years ago, and consisted initially in finding and choosing three hundred glass objects from every major period in glass history. I searched for varying origins and styles to reflect the diversity of glassmaking techniques and many kinds of animals. I wrote to museums, manufacturers, and galleries all over the world, and was often aided by helpful curators who guided me in the selection of pieces that best displayed the representation of animal forms in glass.

Why has mankind long created likenesses of animals in glass? There are any number of likely reasons, and in the course of my research I have come up with some possible answers. Certainly the choice of animals related to man's attraction to, fear, or outright dislike of a particular creature. Consider, for example, the domestic cat, *felis catus.* The ancient Egyptians venerated it for protecting their stores of grain against small vermin, whereas during the Middle Ages the cat was vilified for its association with paganism and Satan. Just as frequently, artisans depicted animals native to their country. In sixth- to eighth-century Syria, flasks were made in the shape of dromedaries, that able moving transporter of people and cargo. Or in eight- and nineteenth-century Bohemia, a heavily wooded country rich with game, we find goblets

Peacock Window
c. 1910.
Tiffany Studios (United States). Height: 83.8 cm, width: 61.0 cm. Private collection. Courtesy Christie's, New York

Originally used only in public or religious buildings, stained glass entered private homes, thanks to Tiffany. This peacock with its luxurious spread tail filled the home of H. O. Havemeyer, America's first great collector of Impressionism and of Tiffany glass.

etched with depictions of hunting scenes, leaping stags and hounds at the chase. The animal as symbol has carried great import through the ages, such as in the ancient Egyptian deification of a female hippopotamus representing childbirth and fertility, or in the coat of arms of Imperial Russia, the eagle, engraved on a Russian glass teapot of the eighteenth century. Sometimes animals were created in glass simply because they were popular (there are hundreds of depictions of birds from all over the world and all through time, for example) or because their form was so well suited to the prevailing art in vogue. For Louis Comfort Tiffany, the rich gradations in color of a peacock feather could be beautifully transformed in his favrile glass, with its iridescence, and in the crisp lines of a cricket or the economical shape of a fish René Lalique adapted his Art Deco designs.

Contributing to the myriad varieties of animals in glass were the materials available to artists at a given time or place. What sensuous patterned pieces could be realized first in mosaic would change altogether when cast in translucent glass. Or a bird engraved on English crystal in the late 1600s ascends to a lush brilliance in stained-glass windows, such as those made by the American John La Farge in the 1880s.

Domestic or wild, observed in nature or created from fantasy, here are the animals of man's making over 3,500 years. My hope is that the reader will take pleasure not only in finding a favorite animal or object here or there, but in tracing how keenly artists have responded with imagination and sensitivity to the natural world around them, and out of it spun their marvelous fantasies in the dazzling world of glass.

Swallow 1932.
René Lalique for Cristal
Lalique (France). Satin
crystal. Height: 15.5 cm.
Courtesy Lalique, Paris

GLASS BEFORE A.D. 500

Although the origins of glass remain uncertain, scholars theorize that it evolved from sand-based glazes for pottery in Mesopotamia more than thirty centuries before the time of Christ. Figures made of powdered quartz, mixed with fluxing agents and metallic oxides and heated in molds in a process borrowed from metallurgy, were known in Egypt by 2500 B.C. These ceramic-like precursors of glass (similar to the oryx, page 14), valued as highly as gold and precious stones, were used to ornament the jewelry and funerary objects of Egyptian nobility.

In the second milennium B.C., true glass beads were first made, formed by casting, winding, or cutting cross sections of glass rods. These became a staple of trade in the region.

In the fifteenth century B.C., the pharaoh Thutmose III pressed northeast into Syria, bringing back knowledge of advanced Middle Eastern glassmaking techniques. During his reign, glass receptacles for perfumes and unguents (for example, the fish on page 20) first appeared in Egypt. Like Syrian vessels, they were made by core-forming: a mixture of clay and dung was shaped to the desired form around the end of a metal rod, then wrapped with overlapping coils of viscous glass. The hot form was rolled on a flat stone or marver to shape and smooth its surface, then trailed with threads of bright blue, yellow, or turquoise opaque glass combed or "dragged" into parallel feathery designs. The metal rod was then extracted and, after annealing, the inner core was removed.

By 300 B.C., when Alexandria emerged as the preeminent center of glass manufacture, the Egyptians had learned how to make sophisticated inlays and plaques of mosaic glass (such as the Apis bull, page 24). Cast and mosaic creatures such as the ram, hawk, bull, lion, jackal, frog, and fish were often

Lion's Head
Egypt, late period, 1085–332 B.C. Height: 6 cm.
The Louvre, Paris

During this period many decorative elements were being made in molded and cut or carved glass paste. This lion had been used for the adornment of a luxury bed frame, which was finished with a lion muzzle at each side of the head and lion paws for the feet.

depicted on Egyptian glasswares, both as symbolic incarnations of specific gods and as literal observations of nature.

About 50 B.C., Syrian glassmakers discovered that molten glass could be blown into a viscous bubble at the end of a metal tube called a blowpipe. This discovery revolutionized the craft. Now vessels could be formed quickly and easily, by puffs of breath and shaped with simple tools that have remained basically unchanged through the centuries. First, the blower inserts the long metal pipe through a small opening in the beehive-shaped furnace used to melt the mixture of sand, soda, and lime that produces glass. Swirling the rod through the molten mass, he withdraws a gob or "gather" of glass. A quick puff results in a bubble or "parison" at the end of the pipe. Constantly turning the pipe to keep the bubble from sagging, the craftsman uses simple forming tools such as metal shears, wooden paddles, and pincers to create the shape desired. A marver or rolling bench provides a level surface on which to smooth the glass. From time to time, the craftsman reinserts the cooling object into the furnace to keep it at the proper viscosity for working. When the general form of the glass is achieved, a solid metal rod called a pontil is attached to the end of the bubble opposite the blowpipe, and the blowpipe is "cracked off" so that the bubble may be opened and shaped to become a vessel. Handles can then be added. The completed piece is then knocked from the pontil and placed in an "annealing oven" where it is gradually cooled to avoid stress fractures. Examples of blown glass include the Roman mouse and the German pig (page 26).

The Syrians also learned how to blow glass into decoratively patterned molds, and how to cut and engrave it. In the first century A.D., transparent glass rapidly became fashionable throughout the Mediterranean area, supplanting the opaque wares of earlier times.

Syrian glassmaking discoveries coincided with the emergence of the Roman Empire. During the four centuries after the birth of Christ, Rome controlled the Eastern Mediterranean (including Syria itself), Alexandria (still a center for luxury glassmaking), and much of continental Europe. Under the Empire, Syrian glassmakers took their techniques to Italy and northward into the areas of the Rhine and the Seine and as far as Britain. Because glass was fragile, it was more practical to set up furnaces at these distant places rather than to try to ship it over hazardous inland routes. Similarities in style and technique have made it difficult to tell whether a piece of so-called Roman glass was made in Syria, Italy, or in one of the far outposts of the Empire. Regardless, then, of its geographic origin, all glass of this period is called Roman glass.

Throughout the period of the Roman Empire, animal motifs were found on various types of wares. Rather than having symbolic meaning, as in Egpytian culture, animals on glass of the Roman era glass were inspired primarily by nature and the events of everyday life.

Although most Roman glass (especially in the north) was utilitarian, nearly all the complicated techniques of handforming and decorating still in use today were known to glassmakers at the time of the Roman Empire. For example, they were able to fuse together different colored layers of glass, carving away the top layer to reveal cameo-like classic forms in relief. In delicate "cage cups" or diatreta, carved forms remain attached to their background vessels by slender posts of glass. Roman-era glassmakers also blew flasks, bottles, and cups in ornamental molds, such as the Gallo-Roman cup depicting a chariot race (page 29). They employed sophisticated methods of decoration, using copper-wheel and abrasive engraving techniques, as well as enameling. Their methods have not differed drastically from those later used in the nineteenth and twentieth centuries. An outstanding example of Roman enameling skill is the third-century cup depicting an embattled bull and bear (page 30).

In A.D. 350, about a century before the fall of the Roman Empire, its seat moved to Constantinople, a city without an indigenous glassmaking tradition. To supply Roman nobility with glass both utilitarian and luxurious, the nearby Syrian glassmaking cities of Tyre and Sidon furnished Constantinople with glasswares.

Bound Oryx

Egypt, late 18th Dynasty (1400–1300 B.C.). Length: 11 cm. Private collection. Courtesy Christie's, London

The medium of this piece is controversial, attesting to the prevailing uncertainty about the origin of glass. It has been described as "Egyptian blue," a term designating a specific chemical compound. While it can be polished to resemble glass, Egyptian blue has been mislabeled as *pâte de verre* or even faience. Animal forms such as the oryx, similar to the ibex, were popular forms as cosmetic palettes, used for grinding powders. An incarnation of Seth, the god of evil, the oryx is shown with its legs bound and its throat slit. The evil spirits thus warded off, the unguents contained therein ensured their owner's protection and survival.

Recumbent Lion

Egypt, 19th Dynasty, possibly late period after 1320 B.C. Length: 4 cm. The Corning Museum of Glass, New York

Originally set on the edge of a small receptacle, this miniature sculpture is of very fine workmanship. The sober, curving line evokes the strength and wisdom of the King of Beasts. In Egypt, the lion was often represented in pairs, back to back, observers of the solar cycle and the passing day.

Frog Necklace
Egypt, 18th Dynasty
(1567–1320 B.C.).
Dimensions:
1.6 × 2.0 cm. The
Louvre, Paris

A native of humid, swampy regions, the frog abounded on the banks of the Nile. Following the dry winter in Egypt, its throaty song was the harbinger of life. In ancient Egypt the frog, signaling nature's reawakening, was linked to the sun cult and, along with the serpent, to the basic forces that preceded the creation of the world.

Anubis
Egypt, 5th–3rd century B.C. Length: 11.6 cm. The Louvre, Paris. Gift of Louise and Ingeborg Curtis Atherton, 1938

The funerary god Anubis guarded the Egyptian tombs. Having embalmed Osiris, he then became the watcher of the dead. Represented in the shape of a jackal, he prowled burial places and oversaw the journey of the dead. The purity of this object is enhanced by its black color. The glass is molded, cut, and polished. Note the very deep markings delineating the rib cage.

15

Bead in the Form of Two Ducks
Saqqara, probably 18th Dynasty (1567–1320 B.C.) or Roman Empire. Height: 0.8 cm, width: 1.6 cm. The Brooklyn Museum. Charles Edwin Wilbour Foundation

Joined as a pair, these ducks are actually small beads; the hole passes through their bodies and wings. They were found at Saqqara, a town located in the Nile Delta near Memphis. The deep blue glass is striated with threads of white glass. The date of this piece is uncertain because this technique of beadmaking appeared in Egypt during the 18th Dynasty and continued into the Roman era.

Scarab
Egypt, Ptolemaic period, 332–30 B.C. Length of body: 8.2 cm. The Toledo Museum of Art, Ohio. Gift of Edward Drummond Libbey

Probably intended as an inlay for the lid of a sarcophagus, this large, probably unique, scarab symbolized Kephri, the god of rebirth. The scarab was cast in fire sections (body and four legs) in a one-part open mold. The deep blue glass undoubtedly imitated lapis lazuli. Scarabs usually appear as faience amulets.

Tawaret

Egypt, Ptolemaic period, 332–30 B.C. Height: 11 cm. The Metropolitan Museum of Art, New York. Gift of Edward S. Harkness, 1926

With her large, proud belly, Tawaret was the symbol of fertility who assisted at childbirth. She was a much-venerated protective deity, and there are many representations of her standing upright.

Wooden Panel with Glazed Composition Inlay

Egypt, late 4th century B.C. Length: 51 cm, width: 4.5 cm. Ex. coll.: Kofler-Truniger. Courtesy Christie's, London

The tradition of craftsmanship continued along the banks of the Nile, despite the eventual decline of the Egyptian Empire, particularly with regard to ritual and sacred objects. The use of glass paste simulated decoration with semi-precious stones, which were exceedingly rare. The choice of colors was often symbolic: blue represented truth, death, and the gods; green was employed for Osiris, god of life and fertility, and rebirth in the hereafter. This acacia wood panel, taken from the cover of a sarcophagus, is encrusted with hieroglyphs, which are an invocation to Osiris asking him to welcome the deceased.

Ram's Head Pendant
Punic, possibly Carthage, 6th–5th century B.C. Length: 2 cm. The Corning Museum of Glass, New York

Through their extensive trade routes, the Phoenicians spread jewelry throughout the world during this period, especially pearls. Made of opaque white glass, this pendant is an early example of coreformed trailed and tooled work.

Hawk's Head
Iran, from the Azerbaijan region, Persia, 3rd century B.C.–2nd century A.D. Length: 6 cm. The Corning Museum of Glass, New York

This amber, three-dimensional hawk's head was cast and wheel-cut. The rectangular-shaped neck feathers were made by wheel-cutting. Its purpose is unclear: it might have been intended as the end of a scepter or as the base of a *rhyton* or at the end of a throne arm.

Top row: **Toad Amulets**
Egypt, Ptolemaic, possibly late period, 6th–3rd century B.C. Height: 2.0–1.6 cm.
Middle row: **Ram Amulets**
Egypt, Ptolemaic, possibly late period, 6th–3rd century B.C. Length: 2.9–2.0 cm.
Bottom row: **Sphinx Amulets**
Egypt, Ptolemaic, possibly late period, 6th–3rd century B.C. Length: 4.4 cm.
Jackal Amulets
Egypt, Ptolemaic, possibly late period, 6th–3rd century B.C. Length: 2.4–3.7 cm. The Corning Museum of Glass, New York

Amulets were often found wrapped in the bindings of mummies although some were used as hieroglyphic inlays on furniture or on mummy cases. They were crudely cast, and ranged in color and type of glass from opaque white glass to a translucent blue or green; traces of gold foil have also been found.

Ibis
Egypt, 5th–3rd century B.C. Height: 5.7 cm. The Louvre, Paris

The ibis, a bird associated with Thoth, the Egyptian god of writing, science, and language, is a beautiful white wading bird with a black head and tail. It was highly valued as a predator against the serpents and other reptiles in the swamps and banks of the Nile. Cemeteries containing mummified ibis have been found near sites dedicated to the cult of Thoth.

Glass Cosmetic Vessel in Shape of Nile Bulti Fish
Egypt, El Amarna, c. 1350 B.C. Length: 14.5 cm. The British Museum, London

When Amenophis IV established his new capital at El Amarna, the city benefited from the resulting prosperity and the artistic benevolence of the pharaoh and Queen Nefertiti. The earliest mold-formed glass receptacles were immensely popular during the brief and euphoric period when El Amarna was the seat of government and before Thebes regained its predominant position. This burgeoning was short-lived, and objects found on the site of El Amarna are rare.

Hawk's Head
Egypt, Ptolemaic period, 3rd–1st century B.C. Length: 6.4 cm. The Corning Museum of Glass, New York

Cast and glass mosaic techniques were used to create this hawk's head. Here the opaque white glass was in-laid, with precast blue markings, while the red, white, and blue eye was formed separately. This hawk-shaped inlay was probably part of a clasp for a broad collar. The choice of a hawk may have been used to invoke Horus, god of light.

Twenty-eight Fish Tile Fragments
Egypt, probably Alexandria, 1st century B.C.– 1st century A.D. Width: 1.9–6.5 cm. Formerly in the Collection of the Comtesse de Béhague, ex. coll.: Kofler-Truniger. Courtesy Christie's, London

After their conquest of Egypt, the Romans purchased fashionable luxury objects, helping to create new markets for glass-makers. New forms in glass mosaic were introduced: plates, platters, and bowls. These brightly colored fish fragments may have come from dishes.

Fragments of a Plate with Reliefs of Crabs and Other Sea Animals

Greek and Roman, 1st century B.C. Width: 51.9 cm. The Metropolitan Museum of Art, New York. Gift of Henry G. Marquand, 1881

These marine motif fragments are from a plaque found near the Villa of Tiberius on Capri. They are representative of the animal art that was found on many fragments of tableware dating from this period. Here the crab is very faithfully cameo-carved as though it had been captured "alive" in glass.

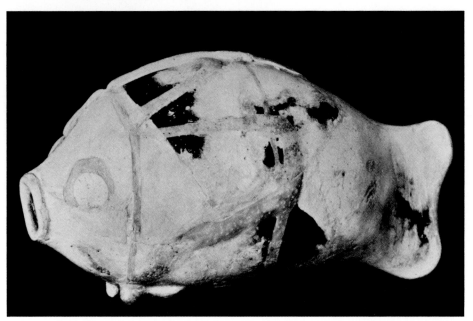

Bottle in the Form of a Fish

Egypt, c. 1403–1347 B.C. Length: 12.5 cm, height: 6.0 cm. Private collection, Germany

Inhabiting the Nile waters in abundance, fish were an accessible and inexpensive source of food, forbidden only to the priests. The fish was considered sacred, and in certain villages there were conflicts between those who wished to eat it and those who regarded it as an incarnation of the god of the sea.

Horus

Egypt, 2nd century B.C.
Height: 15 cm. Musée
Curtius, Liège

Watchful guardians, these
two similar falcons in
molded blue glass have
survived the span of time
with relatively little
damage.

Container in the Form of a Bird

North Italy or Rhineland,
1st century A.D. Height:
6.0 cm, length: 11.7 cm.
The Corning Museum of
Glass, New York

Glassmakers learned to
form glass by blowing
techniques developed
nearly 2,000 years ago.
Blowing produced more
glass at less expense. This
blown-glass bottle held
perfume. In order to use
the scent, it was necessary
to snap off the bird's tail.
The iridescent blue and silver color was caused by the
corrosion which many
glass objects of this period
were subject to.

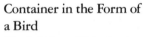

Fish from Revetment Panel

Roman Empire, 1st century B.C.–early 1st century A.D. Length: 17.2 cm, height: 8.2 cm. The Corning Museum of Glass, New York

Made in the mosaic and inlay technique, this fish formed part of a wall revetment panel for a wealthy Imperial house.

Apis Bull Plaque

Roman Empire, possibly Alexandria, 1st century B.C.–1st century A.D. Height: 2.6 cm. The Corning Museum of Glass, New York

The Apis bull cult was especially strong in Memphis, where great attention and ceremonies were conducted whenever a bull died. The bull was traditionally depicted with the sign of the Uraeus between its horns, a cobra poised in a striking position. This is a fine example of flat mosaic glass.

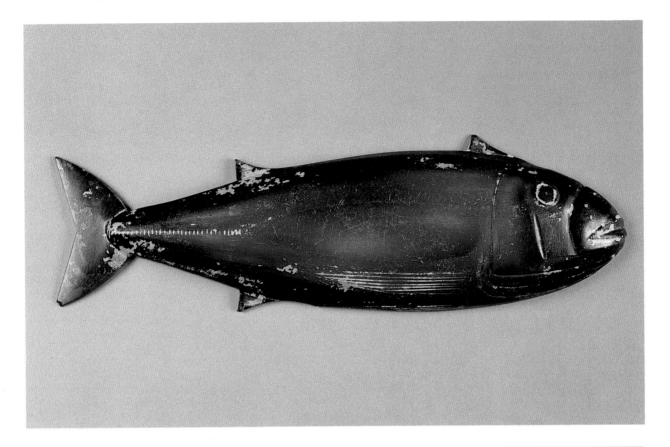

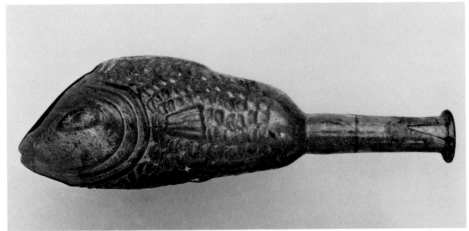

Vase in the Form of a Fish

Roman Empire, n.d. Length: 24 cm. The Metropolitan Museum of Art, New York. Gift of J. Pierpont Morgan, 1917

Fish were an inexhaustible source of inspiration for glassmakers, as evidenced by this pattern-mold-blown bottle. The nacreous-blue color is a result of devitrification. The fish scales in relief are drawn to perfection; the tail forms the neck of the vase.

Dish in the Form of a Fish

Roman Empire, 1st–3rd century A.D. Length: 33.7 cm. The Corning Museum of Glass, New York

Under the Roman Empire, a blown-glass fish was usually quite free in form. This rare example, probably mold-blown or cast and cut, is unique: it is a remaining piece of a luxurious set of tableware. The great value in the object lies in its sculptural contours which give it an aesthetic value over and above its everyday purpose. The surface markings are delicate and elegant, and its deep blue color evokes the depths of Mediterranean waters.

Quadruped
Roman Empire, 3rd–4th century A.D. Length: 13.1 cm. The Corning Museum of Glass, New York

Animal pieces are common in this period, most of them as receptacles, gay and expressive examples of the glassmaker's art. Little altered by time, this attractive, albeit strange, tiny mouse is still translucent. The head and body of the yellowish clear glass mouse were blown and shaped from one bubble; the blue-green eyes, ears, and legs were applied afterward.

Perfume Bottle in the Shape of a Pig
Germany, 3rd century A.D. Length: 9.5 cm. Römisch-Germanisches Museum, Cologne

By the third century, the Roman Empire had attained its greatest extent in the West. Glass whimsies reflected local familiarities, as seen in this perfume bottle, discovered and possibly made at Cologne. With its blown-glass body, the figurine shows how this typical domestic pig, whose visage was likely seen waddling through some Germanic village, was translated into art.

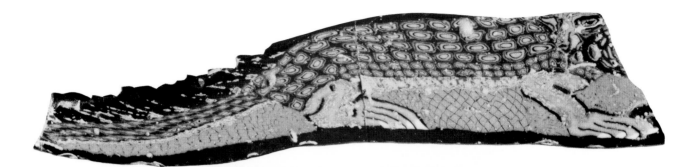

Crocodile Inlay
Roman Empire, Egypt or Italy, 1st century B.C.– 1st century A.D. Length: 8.2 cm, height: 1.6 cm. The Corning Museum of Glass, New York

Made of four different colored canes of glass set in a deep blue mold, this is one of the more magnificent examples of mosaic glass—despite the present condition of the piece.

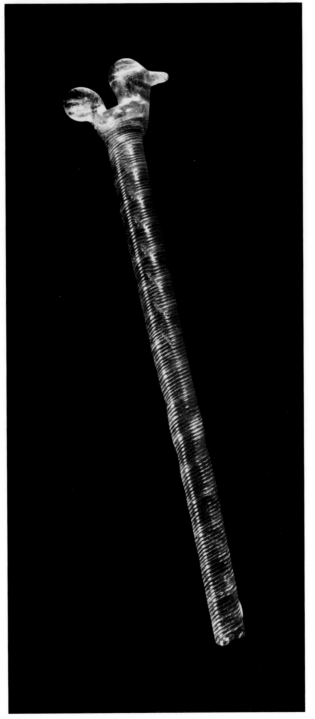

Cock
North Italy, beginning of 2nd century A.D. Length: 18.5 cm. Hungarian State Museum, Budapest

Excavations have revealed many of these small twisted or cabled sticks dating from the Roman Empire, which were possibly the products of local workshops. Lengths of glass rods were twisted and decorated while hot with birds, heads, or other ornaments. One likely theory is that they were used to mix and spread cosmetics. In the nineteenth century they were made into pens.

Birds' Bowl
Roman Empire, first half
of 1st century A.D.
Height: 6.5 cm., diameter: 8.5 cm. The City
Museum, Locarno

Although it was created
over 1,900 years ago, this
bowl is strikingly modern
in style. On the outside are
two birds, probably enameled, possibly cold-
painted, amidst luxurious
foliage; the vivid colors
and the profuse greenery
enliven the dark blue
glass. Few painted objects
of this type dating from
the early days of the Em-
pire have been found.

Rim Fragment of Bowl

Roman Empire, probably Rome, late 1st century B.C.–early 1st century A.D. Length: 12.0 cm, diameter (rim reconstructed): 23.0 cm. The Corning Museum of Glass, New York

An example of wheel-cut glass with an intaglio decoration showing a hen squaring off with a rooster. Barely discernible is the antenna of a bee in the hen's beak.

Bowl with Chariot Race Decoration

Gallo-Roman, 1st century A.D. Height: 6.8 cm, diameter: 8.2 cm. The Rouen Provincial Museum of Antiquities, France

This bowl was probably made in the Rhineland and brought up the Seine valley in the first century. Raised decoration encircles the vessel in three separate bands: an upper border bearing an inscription, a broad central band showing the chariot race, and at the base of the vessel a frieze of nine hares, rabbits, and stags. The cup was first broken by a blow from the pick that unearthed it in 1857 at the Château de Trouville-en-Caux in Normandy. The large chip at the top was caused by its being dropped accidentally.

29

Circus Beaker

Roman Empire, 3rd century A.D. Height: 9 cm, diameter: 10.4 cm. The Danish National Museum, Copenhagen

Combat between bulls, bears, and lions were held in arenas to amuse the public from all over the Empire; frescoes, ceramics, and mosaics testify to the Roman populace's fondness for this form of entertainment, often paid for by the Emperor himself. Enamel work on glass, the technique employed for this beaker, was done from the first century, in Syria, and probably in Egypt and Italy.

Fish
Syria, 3rd–5th century A.D. Height: 7.6 cm, length: 15.2 cm. The Toledo Museum of Art, Ohio. Gift of Edward Drummond Libbey

The struggle of this thick glass fish to escape is conveyed with sculptural force.

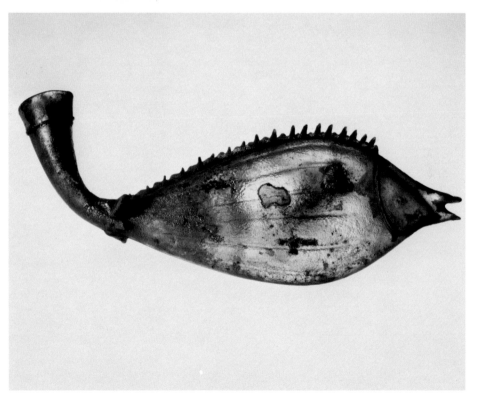

Flask in the Form of a Fish
Roman Empire, probably Syria, c. 3rd century A.D. Length: 12.8 cm. The Corning Museum of Glass, New York

The many fish-shaped flasks to be found in collections of antique glass and museums suggest that they must have been fabricated in huge quantities. This blown and trailed flask has become opaque.

The fins are applied and delicately pincered; the tail is the spout.

MEDIEVAL, ISLAMIC, AND VENETIAN GLASS: A.D. 500-1600

With the fall of the Roman Empire, trade and communication between the Mediterranean regions and northern Europe diminished. Cut off from Roman influence and having lost their market for more sophisticated wares, glassmakers along the Rhine and in France continued to produce relatively crude vessels decorated only with trailed or pincered applications of glass. Few examples of Rhenish or Merovingian glass are known today, in the main because the Christian Church discouraged the pagan practice of burying the dead with their possessions—a tradition that had ensured the survival of many pieces of earlier Egyptian and Roman glass.

It was the Church, however, that kept the light of civilization burning in northern Europe during the Dark Ages. Colored glass for windows—the precursor of stained glass—was found in the monastary at Jarrow, England (A.D. 682–870). The earliest known stained-glass windows are from the eleventh-century cathedral at Augsburg, Germany, but by the twelfth century, stained glass was common throughout northern Europe.

By that time, forest glasshouses along the Rhine and in France were turning out transparent green or grayish common wares (made so by impurities, particularly iron, in the local sand) in characteristic shapes that persisted into the seventeenth and early eighteenth centuries. Called *waldglas* (forest glass) in Germany and Central Europe, and *verre de Fougère* (fern or bracken glass) in France, so named because it was manufactured in regions where wood (for fuel and potash) and fern (an excellent fluxing agent when burned to ash) were abundant, the glass was blown in pattern molds or decorated while hot with applied trailing and pincered blobs, or prunts.

In contrast to the common glass of northern Europe, the Near East continued to produce both fanciful and highly sophisticated wares. Mesopota-

Bird
Near East, possibly Egypt, early Islamic, 7th–9th century A.D. Height: 9.5 cm. The Corning Museum of Glass, New York

With its disproportionate crest and spread wings, this sprightly bird suggests a proud cock with its hackles up. Despite the slight iridescence and the formation of a thin opaque film, light still penetrates the amber-colored glass.

33

mian and Persian craftsmen revived the Hellensitic process of wheel-cutting as a means of faceting and decorating clear colorless glass vessels (see the falcon-and ibex-ornamented cup on page 40), a practice that was further developed in later Islamic glassware, such as the Corning Ewer on page 45. In this technique, rotating stone wheels were used to abrade the surface of a glass object or cut it back to leave a design in relief.

By the eighth century, virtually every nation in the Middle East and northern Africa had been conquered by Arabian armies, and for centuries thereafter, the region was unified under a series of Islamic rulers. During this relatively peaceful and productive time, a great quantity of glass was produced at such centers as Baghdad, Basra, Samarra, Damascus, Aleppo, and Raqqa. Reflecting the Arabic life-style, horse and camel figures were popular (page 37), while sophisticated decorating techniques, including wheel-cutting (page 43), gilding (page 38), enameling (page 42), were widely used. The overriding characteristic of Islamic decoration is the rhythmic repetition of stylized forms, often floral or animal, over the entire surface of an object. Bold, often perfunctory gilding and Chinese-influenced enamel-painted decoration covers the entire surface of the bell-shaped mosque lamps made in Syria, primarily the mosques of Cairo, where they were suspended high above the floor.

Mongol invasions in the fourteenth century brought Chinese influence to bear on other Islamic glass. For example, the large bottle on page 39, is elaborately decorated with Oriental-style motifs. Islamic glassmaking declined after 1402, when the Mongols sacked the major factories in Damascus. With the fall of Constantinople in 1453, Middle Eastern domination of the glassmaking industry came to an end.

By that time, however, the glass industry was well-established in Venice, a prosperous commercial city-state at the crossroads of the Oriental/Western and north/south trade routes of the day. Although glass had been made in Venice for centuries since Roman times, the craft had declined in the Dark Ages, only to be revived in the eleventh century when glassblowers from Constantinople arrived to make mosaics for St. Mark's cathedral. By 1291, there were so many glassblowers' furnaces within the close confines of the city that a decree ordered them removed to the nearby island of Murano. Though organized into guilds and given the privileges of nobility, the Murano glassmakers were literally prisoners, forbidden to leave with their commercially valuable knowledge.

Led by gifted craftsmen like Angelo Barovier, the Venetians excelled in a variety of forming and decorating techniques, including the art of polychrome and gilt enameling (pages 48 and 46). Enameling was done by applying a mixture of fusible colored glass, bound by oil, to the surface of the vessel and then refiring it at relatively low temperatures to fix the decoration. In "cold enameling," which is less durable, the colored compound was not fired, but applied to the glass with a binder of oil or varnish.

In 1500, the Venetian glassmakers developed a formula for an almost colorless soda-lime glass, called *cristallo* after the rock crystal quartz that it resembled. The new glass compound had a long "working time" before it cooled to a solid and was frequently blown into extremely thin-walled vessels and drawn out into threads or ribbons, resulting in the elaborate, often fanciful shapes that became the hallmark of Venetian glass craft (page 55).

The Venetians also made a milk-white glass, *lattimo,* that could be threaded intricately within clear glass to form lacelike *vetro a retori.* For the ancient Roman technique of molding colorful cross sections of glass canes into *millefiori* patterns, they subsituted chevron beads, and they engraved glass with a diamond-tipped stylus.

Risking reprisals, many Murano glassworkers managed to leave their island and set up furnaces in northern regions, spreading the influence of *façon de Venise* glass throughout Europe during the sixteenth and seventeenth centuries. Sometimes Venetian-style decoration is found on local forms (for example, the Bohemian *humpen* on page 52). More often, northern glassmakers copied both Venetian forms and styles so closely (page 51) that, as in Roman times, geographic attribution can be difficult.

In 1574, the Venetian Giacomo Verzelini received a royal patent to produce glass at his Crutched Friars glasshouse in London. Verzelini excelled in diamond-point engraving and his graceful goblets (page 50) whetted the English taste for delicate Venetian-style pieces.

During this time, Venetian artistry in glass was challenged by craftsmen from the Catalonian region of northern Spain, whose wares were widely admired. Glassmakers in the port city of Barcelona were influenced by enameled "Damascus" glass imported from the Middle East, and in the fifteenth and sixteenth centuries they developed a unique mode of enameled decoration— Mudejar, part Spanish, part Moorish—characterized by stylized plant and animal forms (page 54). In the sixteenth century, Venetian-style enameling and diamond-point engraving became popular for decorating local Spanish glass wares (page 47). Spanish-made glass was much sought after for its excellent clarity, which was due to a fluxing agent derived from Barilla, a native salt-marsh plant.

A Double Unguentarium Supported by Two Horses
Near East, possibly Syria, c. 6th–8th century A.D. Height: 11.3 cm. The Corning Museum of Glass, New York

From A.D. 266 to 640, the governors of Persia exerted great pressure against the eastern part of the Roman Empire. The glassmakers of that region catered to the taste of the Sassanides, a Persian dynasty that reigned from the third to the eighth century. The glass was usually clear and bubbled; the appliquéd netting along the neck made it easier to hold. This piece is an unusual variation of the kind of fla-çon for ointments in use along the Syrio-Palestinian coast: two receptacles in one.

Animal-shaped Flask

Eastern Mediterranean, Syria or Palestine, 6th–8th century A.D. Height: 12.7 cm. The Toledo Museum of Art, Ohio. Gift of Edward Drummond Libbey

A cage of glass fillets holds the spherical vase and also affixes it to the dromedary. The glass netting is only attached to the receptacle at a few points and is set on the animal's back much like a packsaddle; the dromedary's legs ensure stability. The bubbled glass is transparent yellow with a few blue fragments.

Bottle in the Shape of a Horse

Syria, early Arabic period, 12th–13th century. Height: 15.2 cm, length: 19.1 cm. The Toledo Museum of Art, Ohio. Gift of Edward Drummond Libbey

In the Arab culture, the horse has both a useful and unostentatious presence. It was the carrier of trade and travel between Byzantium, Persia, and other Arab lands. Never a common pack animal, the horse was carefully nurtured, for it was synonymous with wealth and renown. The choice of this fragile and precious material is unusual in a nomadic society. The body is blown, and the legs and harness are applied.

Glass Shards with Pelicans

Egypt or Syria, 13th–14th century. Width: 7.7 cm. The Louvre, Paris

The pelican is common in Islamic art, probably because of its legendary generosity toward its offspring, and its unselfish behavior during famines. Still discernible in these fragments, the bird, with its white body and red and gold beak, flies over an aquatic vista. The gold, either powdered or leaf, was applied to the glass at the same time as the porcelain enamel, and was fixed by heating. The workshops at Aleppo used this technique until about 1250, and at Damascus until it was destroyed by Tamerlane in 1400.

Glass Shards with Lions

Egypt or Syria, 13th–14th century. Length: 4.0–7.0 cm. The Louvre, Paris

In contrast to European heraldry tradition, the lion rarely appears on coat of arms in the Islamic countries. However, it was the emblem of the Mamluke Sultan Baybars (1260–1277). Blazons of court officials, such as that of the cup-bearer, often appear on vessels of the period.

Bottle

Syria, Mamluke period, c. 1320. Height: 44.5 cm. The Metropolitan Museum of Art, New York. Rogers Fund, 1941

This very large bottle, excellently preserved, is rare enough to have a place in scholarly literature. It is generally believed to have been made in Damascus, where it illustrates the influence of the Chinese at the time of the Mongol invasions. Its circular motifs, continuous frieze, and iconography are suggestive of metal works. This is further confirmed by the fact that metal objects of the late thirteenth century also have the same script and identical styles.

Cup
Iran or Iraq, probably 9th century A.D. Height:
9.2 cm, diameter: 14 cm.
The Corning Museum of Glass, New York

Recent archeological excavations in Iran have uncovered many wheel-engraved crystal glass objects. The Nishapur site in Khurasan, a province in northeastern Persia, has yielded pieces of the highest quality. Samarra, one hundred kilometers north of Baghdad and for a time the capital of the Califs, has also yielded cups, bowls, and other receptacles that carry on animal traditions familiar in pottery since the fourth millennium. On this cup, four birds alternate with four ibexes, an animal always linked with the gods of fertility. On the base, two falcons surround a Tree of Life and two scrolls, the symbol of the victory of day over night.

Bottle
Probably Iran, 9th–10th century A.D. Height: 16.6 cm. The Corning Museum of Glass, New York

The body of this Iranian bottle has been cut back to show in relief three pairs of wild sheep facing each other, separated by geometric motifs. The curved horns and legs accentuate their grace and movement.

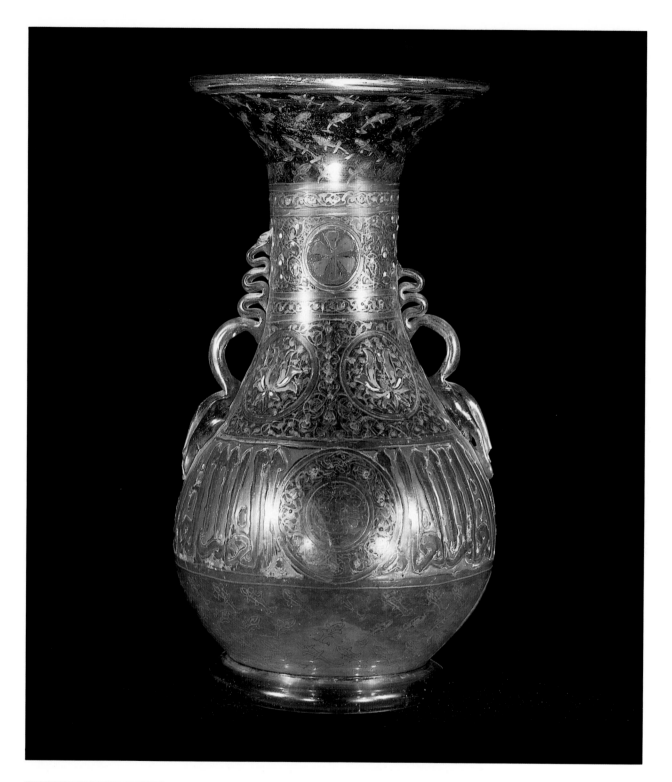

Mamluke Vase
Syria, probably Damascus, 1320–30. Height: 30.2 cm, diameter (greatest body): 16.2 cm. The Corning Museum of Glass, New York

This extremely rare enameled vase has three horizontal bands, the middle of which has spheres on a red-and-gold background set off with touches of thick enameling. The upper and lower bands are decorated with small fish arranged in the shape of chevrons and painted red. Goldfish were considered lucky and were thought to offer protection against accidental death by poisoning.

Egyptian Glass Beaker
Found in Upper Egypt,
c. 14th century. Height:
11 cm. The British Mu-
seum, London

Note the similarity be-
tween this sensitively
wheel-cut beaker and that
made in Syria, page 44.

Fish

Syria, c. 1300. Height:
15.2 cm. The Louvre,
Paris

A garland of flowers and
geometrical motifs sepa-
rate the flared mouth of
this beaker from the tiny
goldfish swimming ran-
domly about. The same
theme, treated in an identical manner, can be found
on objects made between
1290 to 1310, in Syria
and in the south of Russia
as evidence of trade be-
tween those two regions.

Eagle

Syria, mid-13th century.
Height: 12 cm. The
Louvre, Paris

The eagle or falcon, birds
of prey, are the only birds
reproduced on Mamluke
coat of arms. They are intended to represent the su-
premacy of the sultans
and, in a more aesthetic
sense, serve as ornamental
motifs. The eagle, done in
thick red enamel on a
white background, stands
out vividly from the sur-
face of this perfume vial.

The Corning Ewer
Probably Iran, possibly
Egypt, late 10th–
early 11th century A.D.
Height: 16 cm. The Corn-
ing Museum of Glass,
New York

Glass objects of Islamic origin in crystal often re-
count bucolic stories: the
mouflons, ibexes, and
gazelles depicted are sup-
posed to protect villages
and ward off evil. This su-
perb egg-shaped ewer was
blown in colorless glass,
covered with a thin film of
green, and then cut back
at the wheel to the clear
(now translucent) back-
ground to leave only the
extraordinarily precise and
delicate outlines of the
birds of prey attacking
gazelles.

Enameled Tazza
Barcelona, 1560–1600.
Diameter: 22.6 cm. The
Corning Museum of Glass,
New York

Historically, Barcelona has
vied with Venice for su-
premacy in glass. Even in
the court of Rome, Bar-
celona glass competed

with Venetian glass. This
enameled glass tazza is
similar in form, but very
different in decoration
from Venetian work. Aside
from the friezes and a few
details in blue and yellow,
the naive and chimerical
depiction of this hunting
scene is predominantly
green and white.

Plate Decorated with a Portrait and a Border of Vines, Peacocks, and Goldfinches in Flight
mid-15th century. Attributed to Angelo Barovier (Italy). Diameter: 25.6 cm. Provincial Museum of Art, Trente

This plate of a rich amethyst hue is attributed to Angelo Barovier, a master glassmaker, especially of colored glasses. His family had been famous glassmakers on Murano since the thirteenth century. Like all young and wealthy Venetians of his time, Barovier attended the University of Padua. Upon his return, he went into the family business, which had attracted a group of painters, who were friendly with glassmakers. In the center of the plate, the profile of a woman's head was inspired by the "Court of the Queen of Sheba."

Barovier Cup
Mid-15th century.
Formerly attributed to Angelo Barovier (Italy).
Height: 18 cm. Museo Vetrario, Murano

The Venetian glassmakers, a solidly established corporate guild, received many commissions for commemorative pieces. This mar-
riage cup, enameled on blue glass in the Renaissance style of c. 1470–80, comes from the Barovier workshop. Anzolo (Angelo) died in 1460. The portraits of the bride and groom are interspersed with a procession on horseback and a scene of women bathing in the Fountain of Love.

Barbara von Zimmern and Her Arms

Germany, 1518. Height: 63.5 cm, width: 45.1 cm. The Metropolitan Museum of Art, New York. The Cloisters Collection, 1930

The stag is often found depicted in stained-glass Gothic cathedrals as part of scenes from the Bible or the lives of the saints. Its presence may also have had a symbolic meaning. This piece, from a German cloister, probably at Sulz an der Neckau, was a donation from Barbara von Zimmern, who is shown at prayer facing her husband, Wilhelm von Weitingen, depicted on a neighboring panel.

Goblet 1581.
London Glasshouse of
Giacomo Verzelini (England). Height: 20.6 cm.
Victoria and Albert Museum, London

After having worked in
Antwerp for twenty years,
Venetian glassmaker Jacob
Verzelini moved to England in 1572 where Elizabeth I granted him an
exclusive right to fabricate
crystal drinking-glasses for
twenty-one years. Of the
twelve known extant
glasses, eleven, including
commemorative glasses,
were diamond-engraved
outside the glasshouse,
probably by Anthony de
Lysle. Of the eight pieces
extant, this one is thought
to be a marriage glass. The
traditional upper frieze
shows a stag, a unicorn,
and two dogs. The lower
portion of the goblet has
three medallions with the
inscriptions "John-Jone,"
"Dier–1581," and the coat
of arms of Elizabeth I.

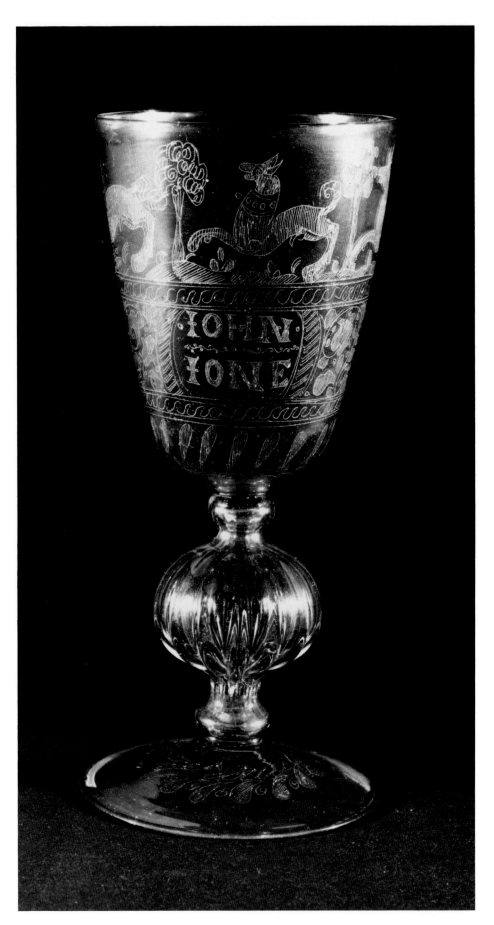

Jug with Handle
Bohemia, 1592. Height:
17.8 cm. The Toledo Museum of Art, Ohio. Gift of
Edward Drummond Libbey, 1950

Bohemia, a land thick
with forests, became a part
of the Hapsburg Empire in
1526. Its glassworks had
been famous since the
fourteenth century, and at
the urging of the Imperial
Court they began to compete with those of Venice.
The pitchers from both
sources are alike in form,
usually without the lids.
Understandably, hunting
scenes were a common
motif: here, two dogs pursue a red stag. The fabrication date is usually
mentioned.

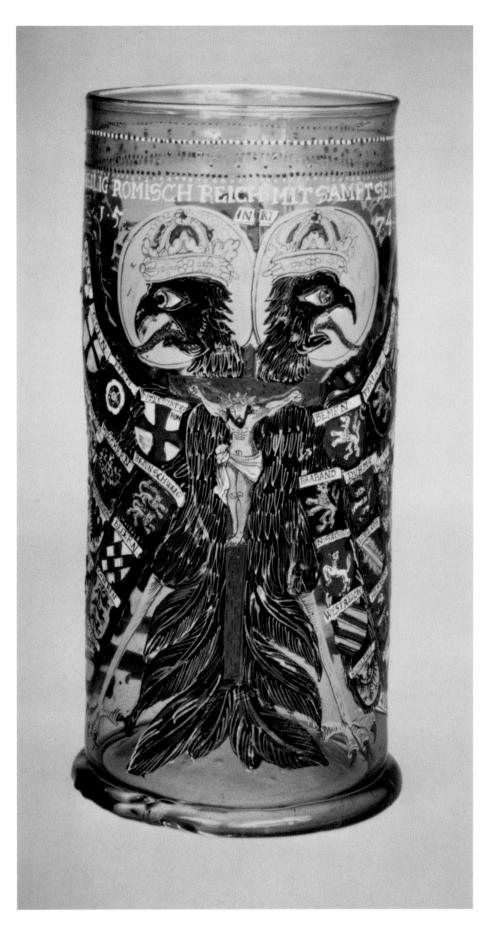

Reichsadler Humpen
Bohemia, 1574. Height: 26.4 cm, diameter (rim): 12.7 cm. The Corning Museum of Glass, New York

The two-headed eagle symbolized the unity of the Germanic Holy Roman Empire. The German emperors and princes, who deemed themselves the heirs of Rome, assumed the symbol of the Roman legions in the eleventh century and incorporated it into their coat of arms. Later, the crucifix was replaced by an orb, with or without a cross on top. Called *humpen,* these beakers were actually used for drinking and were displayed on shelves according to size. Drinking was an act of much importance—virtually a ritual—and the quality of the vessel was more important than that of its contents.

Footed Hunting Goblet
Bohemia, 1597. Height: 27.2 cm. The Corning Museum of Glass, New York

As the demand for enameled glass waned in Venice, there continued a market for it in northern Europe, eventually served by enamelers in Bohemia. This particular goblet is typical of those made between 1590 and about 1610. The pastoral hunting scene that wraps around the top portion of the goblet depicts one of the more common scenes in glass of this origin.

Flask
Spain, c. 1550. Height:
20.6 cm. The J. Paul
Getty Museum, California

In the sixteenth and seventeenth centuries, the province of Barcelona produced
an enameled glass that derived from two great traditions: those of the
Venetians and the Moors.
This bottle, having a flat-
tened shape like a pilgrim's
flask, is of transparent
glass, with the birds in
polychrome enamel; it is a
fine example of the locally
made products.

Oil Lamp in the Shape of a Horse
Venice, 16th century.
Length: 21.8 cm, height:
12.5 cm. Museo Vetrario,
Murano

Since the Egyptians,
dwellings were lit by oil
lamps. Only in the six-
teenth and seventeenth
centuries were they made
out of glass in Murano.

These light-diffusing vessels took the form of
strangely shaped beasts,
precursors of the Baroque
and its extravagances.
Somewhat improbable on
its frail legs, with its small
head and enormous body,
the horse was blown and
the decoration tooled and
pincered with appreciable
dexterity.

GLASS OF MANY NATIONS: 1600-1840

In the two and one-half centuries covered by this chapter, glassmaking progressed from the handworked furnaces of the European forests to the factories of New England, where mechanical pressing techniques allowed the rapid duplication of inexpensive decorative wares for a middle-class market.

In sixteenth- and early seventeenth-century Germany and Bohemia, the Venetian decorative influence remained strong, but the sturdy *waldglas* forms and a new lime-potash glass that favored engraving gradually became Germanic specialties. Other such Germanic forms include the *Roemer,* with its broad bowl, conical foot, and prunts (pages 68 and 69); the *passglas,* a tall, copious beaker marked off at intervals with decorative bands so that each person to whom it was passed could quaff his share (page 62); and the large, cylindrical, ceremonial *humpen,* some of which were made in Venice for decoration in Germany (page 66).

Local variations of *façon de Venise* glass, with its decorative threading, and snake-and-dragon stems (page 70), also appeared in the Low Countries of Holland and Belgium (where diamond point engraving was especially popular).

Around 1676, at his glasshouse in Henley-on Thames, England, merchant George Ravenscroft discovered that the addition of lead oxide to the glass formula yielded a material that was softer, clearer, and more brilliantly refractive than Venetian soda-lime glass. Ravenscroft's new "crystal" lent itself well to cutting and engraving, and could stand alone without need for an embellishment of decoration. Thus, English glass of this period is relatively simple and unadorned. By the second half of the eighteenth century, high British taxes on lead crystal gradually had driven manufacturers to Ireland, where they developed a tradition of faceted cutting that has recently resumed.

Beaker (Ranftbecher)
c. 1820–25.
Workshop Anton Kothgasser (Vienna).
Height: 10.8 cm. Glass-gallery Michael Kovacek, Vienna

Anton Kothgasser, a painter and gilder at the Vienna Imperial Porcelain Factory, was equally interested in glass. He openly borrowed from the creations of the Gottlob Mohn workshop, whose output of enameled and gilded glass was greatly prized at the Austrian Court. For this reason it is extremely difficult to attribute any one piece to a precise workshop and artist. However, this beaker with birds is a motif that can also be found on porcelain pieces made by Kothgasser.

Soon after Ravenscroft's discovery, the manufacture of English-style lead crystal spread to the continent. Since the seventeenth century, French verriers had devoted themselves almost exclusively to the production of mirrors and flat window glass. But in 1764, the Baccarat factory was founded in order to manufacture decorative wares, and in the early 1880s they began to make English-style lead crystal there as well. Lead crystal had already been produced at the Saint-Louis factory (founded 1767) in 1781.

In seventeenth- and eighteenth-century Venice, meanwhile, the Miotti family was turning out characteristic milk glass vessels, many of them decorated in the Persian style (page 75) to appeal to a Mideastern market. Throughout the seventeenth and eighteenth centuries, Murano glassworkers also practiced lampwork, creating whimsical figures by shaping colored rods of glass which had been softened in the heat of the blowtorch, around matrixes of wire. The technique spread to Nevers and elsewhere in Europe, where many of these items were produced during the eighteenth century.

Best known as a porcelain-exporting nation, China also produced some notable glasswares during the Ch'ien Lung period, from 1736 to 1795. Glass had been made and used in China since about 1000 B.C., but it remained secondary to the ceramic tradition until the eighteenth century, when craftsmen adapted the techniques of jade-carving to cased glass (pages 77 and 78). Insect, fish, and animal forms are often found on the small vases and snuff bottles that lent themselves to this painstaking method of decoration.

To make a "blank" (undecorated form) for cameo-carving, the craftsman may dip a blown bubble of one color into a pot of another color; or he may form a cup of colored or colorless glass, blowing into it a bubble of a contrasting color. The two layers adhere and are then worked as one. After annealing, the outer layer or "casing" of glass is carved away with hand tools or rotating wheels of stone, copper, or emery. (A century later, cameo glass craftsmen learned to remove unwanted portions of the outer casing with a bath of hydrofluoric acid before hand- or wheel-finishing.)

Early in the nineteenth century, a class of well-to-do burghers emerged in Germany, Bohemia, and Austria. They provided a ready market for decorative glass of the so-called Biedermeier style, including goblets, tankards, and vases. Heavy and thick, such pieces were often decorated with gold rims and engraved or enameled with scenes or animal figures (pages 56 and 72).

In America, glass had been made since 1608, when the Jamestown, Virginia, colonists established a short-lived factory on the James River. In the

Figurine
France, 18th century.
Height: 13 cm. Musée des
Arts Décoratifs, Paris

Known as *verre de Nevers,*
this drawn glassware first
appeared in the sixteenth
century when enamel
workers trained at Murano
amused themselves at their
workbench lamps by creat-
ing figurines. Of particular interest were the
religious objects, which
people avidly collected to
create their own nativity
tableaux, as well as more
plebeian figures, such as
this butcher with his
duck. Each piece was spun
by hand. Rods of glass of
varying thicknesses were
heated in the flame from
the blowlamp and mod-
eled around an armature of
wire. Colored, opaque, or
transparent glass was used
for the clothing and face.

1820s, however, a new era in glassmaking began when a technique for the
mechanical pressing of hot glass was developed in Pittsburgh, Boston, and at
Sandwich, Massachusetts. About the same time, new methods for blowing
glass into hinged iron molds in various American factories encouraged the
mass production of pressed tablewares and flat mold-blown bottles known as
"American historical flasks." These were usually decorated with patriotic
emblems and political motifs (page 76), including eagles.

Flaçon with Bird Motif
France, 1721. Height:
18 cm. Musée des Arts
Décoratifs, Paris

In the early eighteenth
century, French glass-
makers vied with one an-
other to improve the
quality of their enamel
work. Each workshop in-
vented new methods, ap-
plied for patents, and
petitioned the king for exclusive rights. The glassmakers' guild was beset
with claims, counter-
claims, and court cases to
decide rights and impose
fines. The freshness and
sparkle of the colors on this
flask attest to the quality
achieved in the midst of
such disturbance and
turmoil.

Engagement Glass
Normandy, France, 1740.
Height: 10.4 cm, diame-
ter: 9.5 cm. Musée de
l'Ancien Havre, France

The stained-glass windows
of the Gothic cathedrals
are the glory of chiefly
French glassmakers.
However, in the eigh-
teenth century the tradi-

tion could still be
glimpsed in charming and
cheerful glassware, such as
glasses decorated with
some simple subject. Here
an example with a bird
and flowers, and with a
short saying offering a
toast to a happy marriage:
*Aimons-nous puisque c'est
notre goût* ("Here's to the
good taste of love").

61

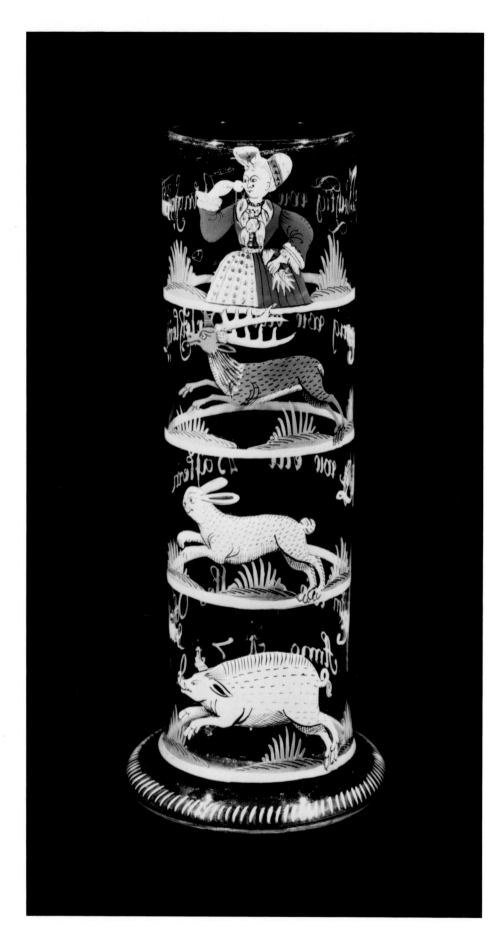

Passglas
Germany, 1719. Height: 25.5 cm. The Corning Museum of Art, New York. Gift of Edwin J. Beinecke

Passglas is the name given to German drinking glasses that are decorated with equidistant horizontal bands marked by a ring of appliquéd or painted glass. They were filled with beer and passed from person to person, each customer drinking his apportioned share. Enameled figures were sometimes painted between the bands depicting animals, playing cards, or anecdotal scenes.

Cup 1665.
Possibly Johan Schaper
(Germany). Height:
6.5 cm, diameter: 6.5 cm.
The Toledo Museum of
Art, Ohio. Gift of Edward
Drummond Libbey

In stained glass, grisaille
painting was used begin-
ning in the Middle Ages to
depict features. Johan
Schaper, a decorator living
in Nuremberg, began to
use it on glasses between
1660 and 1667. Working
on a black enamel back-
ground, he scratched out
details with a needle and
occasionally enhanced the
drawing with colored and
sometimes transparent en-
amels. His favorite sub-
jects were landscapes and
battle scenes. This cup
may have been allegorical,
inspired by some event or
anecdote in the Thirty
Years' War or by the re-
ligious conflicts between
Catholics and Protestants.

**Bottle in the Shape of a
Rabbit**
The Netherlands, c. 1600.
Height: 14.6 cm, length:
17.3 cm. German Na-
tional Museum, Nurem-
berg. Gift of Dr. Wolf
Attenburg, 1881

This strange-looking rab-
bit turned into a bottle is
evocative of tavern life in
northern Europe, such as
the rowdy carousing por-
trayed in a Breughel
painting.

Trick Drinking Glass

The Netherlands, 17th century. Height: 13 cm. City Museum, Cologne

Fabricated in the Netherlands or Germany, the trick drinking glass was very popular in the early seventeenth century. The object was intentionally designed to be difficult to use. Strong drink was to be swallowed down all at once or the drinker would become drunk. Such receptacles often took the form of shoes, horns, pistols, and animals. This standing dog has the comic look of a show dog, with a rosette on its chest and a ruff—the cheery image of a clown.

Schnapps Flask

Germany, 17th century. Length: 15.8 cm, height: 10.5 cm, width: 6.7 cm. Württembergisches Landesmuseum, Stuttgart

Traditional since the Middle Ages, the brandy carafe amused the bourgeoisie of the seventeenth century. It took many droll and original forms, like this fat little piglet with legs. Such models were still to be found in domestic use into the eighteenth and nineteenth centuries.

Mule

Spain, 18th–19th century. Length: 17.8 cm. Victoria and Albert Museum, London

In the towns and villages of the sixteenth and seventeenth centuries, the mule was a familiar sight. Saddled, it offered its best in the service of the upper classes; laden, it was a modest beast of burden. However it was used, it had a reputation for stubbornness and physical endurance. This mule, standing foursquare, with its ears erect, seems determined to stay put.

Bottle (detail of base)

Bohemia, c. 1730. Height: 9.8 cm, diameter: 6.2 cm. Cooper-Hewitt Museum, New York. Gift of the Misses Hewitt

On the bottom part of a flask for perfume or toiletries, this hunting scene is an unusual one for such an object. This is an example of *zwischengoldglas,* double-walled gold glass. An inner glass, exactly ground to fit into a bottomless outer glass, is gilded and engraved, then sealed into the outer glass with colorless resin. The scene is thus imprisoned between two layers of glass.

65

Beaker
Germany, 1678. Height: 18.9 cm. Glassgallery Michael Kovacek, Vienna

Painting on glass was a huge success in Europe, and particularly in Vienna. Covered with enamel, this *humpen* takes up a popular political theme of the time: cavalcades of the ecclesiastical and secular Electors of the Holy Roman Empire, bearing medallions of their native towns.

Siphon
Germany, 17th century.
Height: 30.8 cm. Musée
Curtius, Liège

In northern Europe from
the sixteenth through the
eighteenth century, small
glassworks were located in
wooded mountain regions.
In part, they produced
such pieces as this siphon
or trick glass. The liquid
must be drunk from the
opening in the stag's head.
It is evidence of the high
degree of technical skill
that obtained in such forest glassworks.

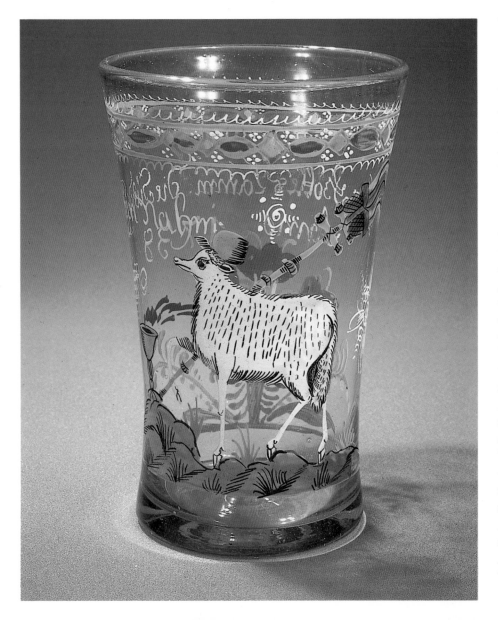

Beaker (Easterglass)
Bohemia or Bavaria, 1738.
Height: 16.4 cm. Glass-
gallery Michael Kovacek,
Vienna

Animals were extremely
popular subjects for en-
amel paintings on glass in
the seventeenth and eigh-
teenth centuries. Domestic
animals—horses and
dogs—as well as animals
of the forest and mountain
animals—stags and ea-
gles—are found in scenes
of warfare, hunting, and
daily life. The animal
could also be highly sym-
bolic, as is the case with
this "Lamb of God," a
symbol of sacrifice. The
lily-of-the-valley and the
frieze of stylized flowers
soften the otherwise som-
ber theme and its implica-
tions. The date of
fabrication of this fine enamel piece is engraved, as
is the inscription: "*Das
Gottes Lamm, die Süden hin
Nahm*" ["The Lamb of God
Taketh Away all Sin"].

Dog (liquor bottle)
South Germany, 17th cen-
tury. Height: 11.5 cm.
The Corning Museum of
Glass, New York

Another fine example of
bottles in popular shapes
(who doesn't like dogs?)
used to hold liquor.

Beaker
Possibly Bohemia, 1729.
Height: 10.9 cm. Glass-
gallery Michael Kovacek,
Vienna

The naive charm of illus-
trated German drinking
glasses is likewise an in-
dication of amateur craftsmen. Working with
enamel on glass was a popular hobby in the seven-
teenth and eighteenth
centuries. Domestic or historic events, hunting
scenes, caricatures of contemporary society and
morals—all manner of
things were revealed in
glass. The fox preaching to
the geese is an image of
the authority of the
Church over the faithful:
"If you don't listen atten-
tively, I shall gobble you
up. 1729."

Goblet
Probably the Netherlands,
c. 1670–85. Height:
32.7 cm. The Corning
Museum of Glass, New
York

In the Netherlands, *façon
de Venise* was given its most
extravagant expression in
this serpentine goblet. The
base consists of a ribbed
stem, twisted and wound
around the stem, to which
a crest and blue wings have
been attached. Such
forms, ever more elaborate
and ill-suited for use, testify to the fantasy and vir-
tuosity of these expatriate
glassworkers.

**The Fire of St. Rombaut
Tower at Malignes,
Belgium** 1687.
Probably Verreries de
Bruxelles (Belgium).
Height: 16 cm. Musée
Curtius, Liège

A pastoral scene very
much in the manner of
Breughel, this diamond-
point engraving shows
town life *circa* 1690; a
popular saying is engraved
along the upper border.
The animal symbols of the
spiritual and the worldly
life are shown as well.

Flaçon in the Form of Two Mice

c. 17th century.
Bonhomme Glasshouse
(Belgium). Length:
10.8 cm, width: 4.5 cm.
Musée Curtius, Liège. For-
merly A. Baar Collection

Liège glassmaking reached
its height under the impe-
tus of the Bonhomme
brothers. The glassworks
they opened in 1638 bene-
fited from some important
technical improvements:
quality raw materials and
coal-burning furnaces.
Italian and German
workers were employed to
produce glass in the Venetian and English style, as
well as in the local ones.
The shapes created were
therefore highly varied, as
in this odd carafe. It is
hard to tell which genre
produced this two-headed
Siamese mouse.

Trick Goblet

Northern Europe, late
17th–early 18th century.
Height: 30.8 cm. The
Corning Museum of Glass,
New York. Gift of Jerome
Strauss

Beautiful to look at, dia-
bolically difficult to figure
out just how to quaff the
contents—trick goblets
made at this time required
more patience than thirst
from drinker.

Dog 1820.
Anton Kothgasser
(Vienna). Height:
11.0 cm. Ex. coll. Krug.
Courtesy Sotheby's,
London

One of Anton Kothgasser's
innovations was the use of
gilded or silver-stained
borders. His pieces are
signed with his name and
initials and sometimes
even his Vienna address.
The black inscription on
the edge of this glass gives
the following information:
"The painter lives in Spanish Spitalberg, at No.
227, in Vienna, Anton
Kothgasser." The allegorical figure of a dog with a
helmet and sword repre-
sents fidelity, the theme of
the picture.

Goblet c. 1763–64.
Enameled by William
Beilby (England). Height:
25.4 cm. Whitehaven
Museum, England

The art of enameling on
glass in England owes
much credit to the pro-
digious talents of the
Beilby family. The elder
Beilby was responsible for
seeing to it that his four
children were well edu-
cated in glassmaking, and
eventually his son William
distinguished himself as
the leading enameler in
the family. This goblet
bears the coat of arms of
King George III, and on
the other side the following legend is inscribed:
"Success to the African
Trade of Whitehaven." It
seems that the goblet was
to commemorate the
launching of the *King
George,* on its mission to
bring more slaves to En-
gland. Interestingly
enough, the third mate on
board was John Paul Jones,
founder of the U.S. Navy.

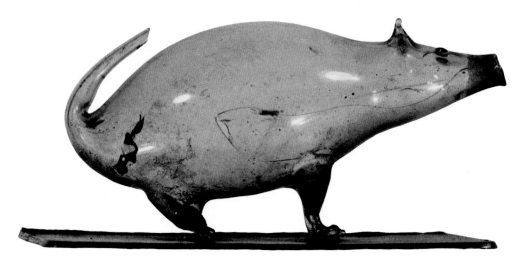

Perfume Bottle in the Form of a Mouse
France, early 19th century. Length: 7.7 cm. Musée International de la Parfumerie, Grasse, France

Found at Grasse, the land of intoxicating perfumes and subtle fragrances, this tiny mouse is a sample bottle for perfume. When perfume bottles were largely made in porcelain and crystal, this little piece of blown glass was viewed as quite ordinary and unpretentious.

Bottle and Two Tumblers 1730–35. Miotti Glasshouse (Venice). Height (bottle): 27.5 cm, (tumblers): 8.6–8.7 cm. The Corning Museum of Glass, New York

This *lattimo* glass was decorated in a fashion calculated to appeal to the Middle Eastern market, interested at that time in exotic, arabesque patterns. The choice of parrots was characteristic of works by the Miotti factory.

◄

Horse
France, late 18th century. Length: 17 cm, height: 16.3 cm. Musée de Grasse, France

Unglamorous but untiring, the small glass factories of Provence continued to produce. The massive form of this horse gives it a medieval aspect, but its manufacture points toward more modern times. It is robust, like the small horses used in those days to transport goods around the countryside.

Vase in the Shape of a Fish
China, Ch'ien Lung period (1736–1795). Length: 17.9 cm, width: 13.7 cm. Museum of Fine Arts, Boston. Bigelow Collection

This fish-shaped vase is a masterful, accomplished example of the Chinese cameo glass tradition.

Unusual Green Peking Glass Tripod
China, Ch'ien Lung period (1736–1795). Height: 10.8 cm. Courtesy Ralph M. Chait Gallery, New York

During the reign of Emperor Ch'ien Lung, the European market was inundated with Peking glass. At the time, the taste ran to small objects in cameo glass. This tripod bowl with its precious coloring shows the painstaking work of the Chinese artisans. Chih Lungs are baby dragons, so called because of their divided tails and lack of claws.

Left: **Jackson American Eagle Flask** c. 1828. Probably John Taylor & Co. (United States). Height: 17.0 cm. The Corning Museum of Glass, New York
Right: **Jackson American Eagle Flask** c. 1824–28 John Robinson & Co., Stourbridge Flint Glass Works (United States). Height: 15.9 cm. The Corning Museum of Glass, New York

Figured flasks had their heyday in American life for about fifty years, dating from the mid-1820s into the 1870s. Often sold as promotional pieces by liquor retailers, the decor generally broke into two camps: historical and pictorial motifs. Both flasks pictured here fall into the former category. The American eagle was made a national emblem in 1782, and the Andrew Jackson flask may well have been created as a give-away object to would-be voters. Apparently it didn't hurt: in 1828 Jackson was elected president.

Vase

Chinese, Ch'ien Lung period (1736–1795). Height: 17.4 cm. Victoria and Albert Museum, London. Salting Bequest

At the end of the eighteenth century, the Chinese regarded glass as a substitute for such semiprecious stones as agate and jade. Snuff bottles, very popular today in the art market, are one refined example. Most of these polychrome glass articles draw inspiration from nature. Carved on a wheel, the shrimp on this vase, which is famous among collectors, stands out among the lotus flowers against a turquoise background.

Mouse

Probably England, 18th century. Height: 25 cm. Victoria and Albert Museum, London

The furtive and busy companion of this anonymous eighteenth-century glassmaker was also his model. The artist was inspired by the long thin tail, the last thing usually to be glimpsed of a mouse before it slips quickly into its hole.

Bottle in the Shape of a Bird

Spain, 17th–18th century. Height: 10.3 cm, width: 7.6 cm. The Metropolitan Museum of Art, New York. Gift of James Jackson Jarves, 1881

This bird probably contained rosewater or a light scent. Indeed, the use of perfume was a must in the seventeenth and eighteenth centuries for both men and women. Hygiene was fairly basic, and a good dousing of perfume often replaced any other physical *toilette*.

Engraved Russian Teapot

Russia, St. Petersburg, mid-18th century. Height: 14.5 cm. Ex. coll.: Krug. Courtesy Sotheby's, London

The two-headed eagle joins the "EP" monogram of the Empress Elizabeth Petrovna, daughter of Peter the Great and Catherine I of Russia. The two heads symbolize the Empire and enhance the eagle's significance: imperial sovereignty.

GLASS IN THE AGE OF ART AND INDUSTRY: 1840-1914

The three-quarters of a century after 1840 saw the full flowering of the industrial revolution in Europe and America, the acceleration of technical and scientific discoveries, and improvements in transportation and communication that helped disseminate trends and styles internationally. It also saw the revival of interest in historic cultures and medieval handcrafts, spurred by the teachings of English design philosophers John Ruskin and William Morris.

Against the backdrop of these developments, glass production proceeded along two parallel but philosophically opposing paths from the mid-nineteenth century to the outbreak of World War I. On the one hand, advances in molding and pressing techniques encouraged the mass production of decorative and table wares for the middle classes, particularly in Britain and America. Animal figures were produced at many of these factories. At Atterbury & Company of Pittsburgh, for example, milk glass boxes shaped like ducks (page 85) or surmounted by cats (page 84) were popular, while in England, pressed glass firms including Sowerby, J. Derbyshire, and Burtles Tate offered animal figurines as stock novelty items.

On the other hand, among the well-to-do there was a widespread demand for "art glass"—individually crafted vases, bowls, and plaques that showed off the glassmaker's skill. Glasshouses in England, France, Bohemia, and America vied with one another to produce these wares, using a range of sophisticated finishing and decorating techniques that included casing (coating one layer of glass with another in a contrasting color), acid-etching, copper-wheel engraving, lampworking, and cameo-cutting. The molten glass was treated with various metallic oxides to create special colors and finishes.

Beginning with London's Crystal Palace Exhibition in 1851, "An Exposition of the Art and Industry of All Nations," a series of World's Fairs (at London in 1862; Paris in 1867, 1878, and 1901; Philadelphia in 1876; Chicago in

Vase with Three Handles 1894. Daum (France). Height: 25 cm. Daum Collection

Inspired by Kabyle (Algerian) pottery, this blue-green three-handled vase takes to the light and creates an evocative aquatic atmosphere. The sky, which blends with the pond and water lilies, is remindful of Japanese drawings.

1893; Turin in 1901; St. Louis in 1904) provided glassmakers with a showcase for their best goods. Visitors to these fairs were exposed not only to glass, but to the design traditions of such exotic and faraway cultures as Japan and Turkey. In particular, the Japanese pavilion at the London Exhibition of 1862 had a far-reaching effect on decorative arts for the remainder of the century. Traditional Japanese motifs—cranes, chrysanthemums, and dragonflies—began appearing on French, British, and American art glass, including pieces by Louis Comfort Tiffany (page 102) and Emile Gallé (page 105). Camels and other Middle Eastern subjects were enameled on opaque glasswares such as the vases of the Mt. Washington Glass Company in Massachusetts and the "Queen's Burmese Glass" of England's Thomas Webb & Sons.

Paperweights enclosing lampworked animal figures and flowers enjoyed a vogue at midcentury. These were made at the French factories of Baccarat, Clichy (page 92), and Saint-Louis, as well as at the New England Glass Company and The Boston & Sandwich Glass Company.

Colored and cased glass remained in style throughout much of this period. In the 1870s, glass craftsmen such as John Northwood and George Woodall of the Stourbridge area in England, pushed the techniques of cameo-cutting glass to new heights of technical proficiency. Acid-etching (dipping a cased-glass object into a solution of hydrofluoric acid in order to erode away unprotected portions of its surface) and copper-wheel engraving on clear and cased crystal were decorating techniques throughout the second half of the century.

From 1890 until the First World War, Art Nouveau held sway as the dominant decorative movement in glass. Characterized by flowing, sinuous curves and stylized motifs drawn from nature, the Orient, and medieval times, the Art Nouveau aesthetic was adopted by glassmakers in America and abroad. Emile Gallé of Nancy was the movement's best-known French practitioner, producing a wide range of objects ornamented with insect and animal forms (page 101). René Lalique used acid-etched glass along with gold and precious stones in creating some remarkable pieces of jewelry around the turn of the century (page 107). In the United States, Louis Comfort Tiffany translated the Art Nouveau aesthetic into a stunning series of iridescent vases (page 111) and stained-glass windows and lamps.

The Frenchman Henry Cros, who worked at the Sèvres porcelain factories, revived the ancient Egyptian technique of grinding glass to a powder and melting it in a mold. His *pâte de verre* plaques (page 110) set the stage for further experimentation in this medium by French craftsmen Almeric Walter and François Décorchemont (page 108).

Cologne or Scent Bottle in the Shape of an Elephant
Probably United States (New England or South Jersey) or possibly Europe, c. 1830–75. Height: 12.4 cm. The Corning Museum of Glass, New York

During the rage for figural bottles made in the mid-1800s, ideas for forms covered all manner of American iconography: log cabins, corn, Indians, the Liberty Bell, and popular animals—regardless of their native terrain. Whether filled with liquor, smelling salts, or cologne, the bottles were an inexpensive collectible. Like everything else today, they can be quite costly, especially those with more ornate workmanship, as shown here.

Bear Grease Jars
c. 1870–85.
The Boston & Sandwich Glass Company (United States). Height: 9.8 cm. The Corning Museum of Glass, New York

The shape of this mold-pressed object was thought to have suited its contents: bear grease, which men used to control and coif their hair.

Milk Glass Tureen
United States, 1889.
Height: 17 cm, length:
21 cm, width: 13 cm. Ro-
cle Milk Glass Collection.
Ohio Historical Society

Animal dishes made of
milk glass were made by
various factories—among
them the U.S. Glass Com-
pany; Challinor, Taylor
and Company; and McKee
Brothers—and usually can
be distinguished by such
details as the design of the
base. Top-of-the-line production work was at-
tributed to Atterbury, as
seen in this piece with a
lacework edge.

**Molded Glass Doorstop
in the Form of a Frog**
Ohio (United States),
mid-19th century. Width:
11.1 cm. The Brooklyn
Museum (45.76.3). Gift
of Mrs. Franklin Chace

Made of solid glass, this
aquamarine frog must have
surprised more than one
guest who chanced to en-
counter it serving as a
doorstop, peacefully sit-
ting in the corner. This as-
sembly line product of
molded and pressed glass
was the forerunner of
many inexpensive, mass-
produced, and amusing
articles.

Covered Dish in the Shape of a Duck
c. 1887–90.
Atterbury & Co., Pittsburgh (United States).
Height: 12.6 cm, length: 27.8 cm. The Corning Museum of Glass, New York

Another example of pressed milk and colored glass. These mass-produced objects were popular items in a typical American household.

Dish late 19th–early 20th century.
Valleryshal (France).
Height: 19 cm, length: 28 cm. Musée des Arts Décoratifs, Paris

Amusing tableware, like this hen and her egg-cup chicks, were cheerful objects in the nineteenth-century American home. They were produced in a variety of sizes and colors in opaque or transparent glass.

Covered Vase with Handles (waders) 1877. Cristallerie de Baccarat (France). Height: 21.7 cm. Musée Baccarat, Paris

Shown at the 1878 Paris World's Fair, this lidded vase was inspired by antique Mediterranean forms, while the wheel-engraved motifs reflect the fashion for things Japanese. This piece, which is more decorative than useful, is evidence of the technical prowess of the master glassmakers and engravers.

Pegasus Vase 1882. John Northwood (England). Height: 54.6 cm, width: 34.6 cm. National Museum of American Art, Smithsonian Institution, Washington, D.C. Gift of John Gellatly

The Pegasus vase is the most perfect example of cameo glass in Roman style, which fascinated English glassmakers toward the end of the nineteenth century. Among them were John Northwood, who worked on the vase from 1876 to 1882. The piece consists of a body of dark blue glass cased with a layer of opaque white glass, acid-dipped and carved to reveal the motif in relief.

Snake 1880.
Monot Père et Fils et
Stumpf for Cristallerie de
Pantin (France). Diameter:
7.0 cm. Musée National
des Techniques du
CNAM, Paris

Its body coiled and its
head erect ready to strike,
this tiny snake is one of the
outstanding objects pro-
duced at the Cristallerie de
Pantin. The amber glass
owes its metallic glitter to
metallic copper particles
dispersed in the glass,
which is called aventurine.
Green and red aventurine
are also known. Although
many critics found the
subjects repetitive, they
could not help but admire
the technical innovation,
which earned the com-
pany's glassmakers a *prix
d'honneur* at the 1883
Amsterdam Exhibition.

Serpent or dragon
Probably Venice, c. 1880–1920. Height: 20.9 cm. The Corning Museum of Glass, New York

◄ **Paperweight Enclosing the Figure of a Salamander** c. 1875–80 Possibly Pantin (France). Diameter: 11.5 cm. The Corning Museum of Glass, New York. Gift of the Honorable Amory Houghton

Millefiori colored glass paperweights were in vogue between 1845 and 1855. The French factories of Baccarat, Saint-Louis, and Clichy excelled in methodical production of *millefiori* paperweights; they also produced lively and colorful lampworked motifs of fruits, flowers, butterflies, birds, and snakes. In 1878, the Cristallerie de Pantin exhibited lizard paperweights at the Paris Universal Exposition. This example is amazingly lifelike.

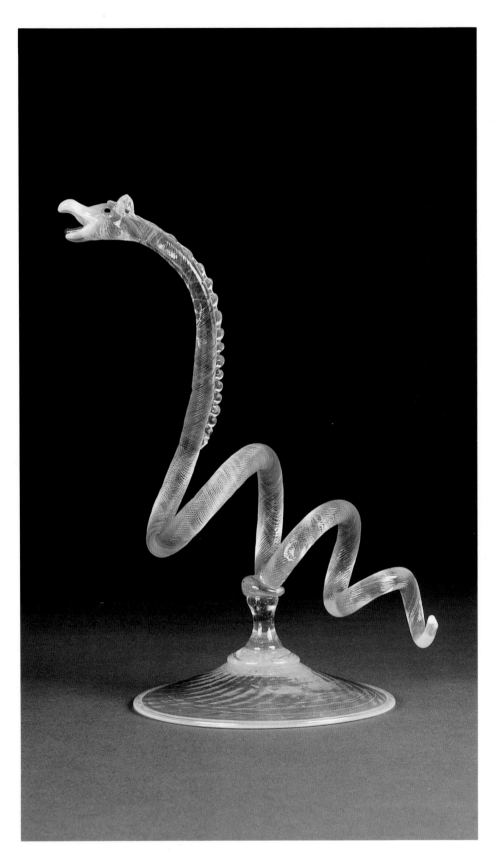

Dog 1847–90. Sandnäs Factory (Finland). Height: 10.5 cm. National Museum of Finland, Helsinki

Of blue glass, this dog is from the small Sandnäs Glassworks at Munsala, on the east coast of Finland. Founded in 1847 by Swedish glassblowers, the company closed its doors in 1890. It produced mainly white and green glass: windowpanes, bottles, and ordinary tableware.

Vase with Handle in the Shape of a Dragon
Venice, nineteenth century. Height: 36.8 cm. The Metropolitan Museum of Art, New York. Gift of James Jackson Jarves, 1881

Giving an animal form to the handle of a vase or a lid was practiced in the middle of the nineteenth century by the Italians. The detailed finishing of the dragon, along with the elegance of line on the transparent turquoise blue over opaque white makes this an outstanding example.

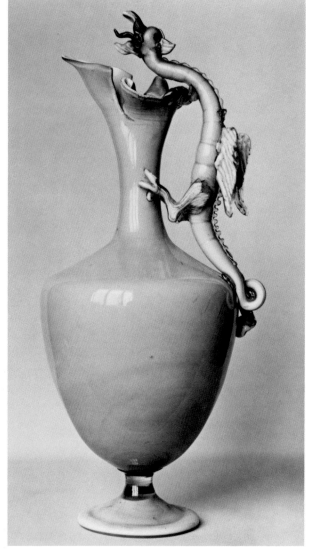

Untitled c. 1880.
Mt. Washington Glass
Company (United States).
Height: 38.1 cm. Minna
Rosenblatt Ltd. Collection

Burmese glass is a kind of
opaque art glass whose
pastel hues shade from
yellow to a salmon-pink.
The surface can be either
matt or shiny. Frederick S.
Shirley of the Mt. Wash-
ington Glass Company
patented Burmese glass in
1885. Shirley presented
Queen Victoria with a
Burmese Service which
popularized the ware in
England, where it was li-
censed to Thomas Webb &
Sons in 1886 as "Patented
Queen's Burmese Ware."
Of significance here is the
Turkish motif on the vase,
influenced by the impact
of Turkish displays at the
1876 Philadelphia Centen-
nial Exposition.

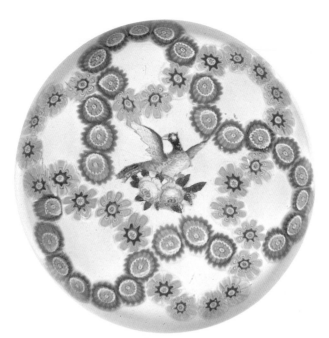

Clichy Paperweight
c. 1846–57.
Verrerie de Clichy (France).
Diameter: 7.9 cm. Courtesy Sotheby's, New York.
Private collection

This rare Clichy paperweight is of particular interest because of the enameled bird with flowers in the center over the opaque white ground.

Fox Paperweight 1871.
Saint-Louis (France).
Length: 12.5 cm. Courtesy Saint-Louis, Paris

After the Franco-Prussian War, the Saint-Louis glass manufacturer was under German management and its name was changed to Saint-Louis Munzthal. At the same time, the fashion in paperweights shifted from *millefiori* to animal figures in molded and frosted crystal.

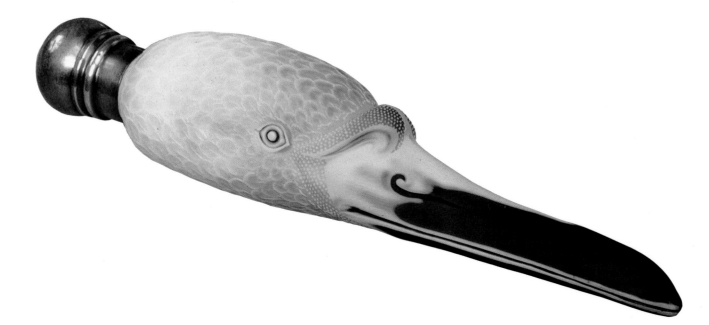

Cameo Scent Bottle
England, c. 1885.
Length: 23.7 cm. Mrs.
Leonard S. Rakow
Collection

At Stourbridge, the glass-making tradition goes back to the sixteenth century and stands at the halfway point between mass-production and individual artistic creation. Local firms turned out finely made, semi-industrial products for the English public, both hand-finished and mechanically decorated. This elegant scent bottle is of opaque white over frosted brown glass, acid-dipped and cameo-carved. The silver cap is stamped with hallmarks of 1885.

Canteen Vase c. 1890.
Possibly Lionel Pearce for Thomas Webb and Sons (England). Height: 20.7 cm. Mrs. Leonard S. Rakow Collection

Glowing and supple, a snake slithers along the contours of the vase, which was acid-dipped and cameo-carved. An octopus, symbol of the underworld, cohabits with the snake in this contradictory environment. Thomas Webb was well known for the quality of his work in cameo glass.

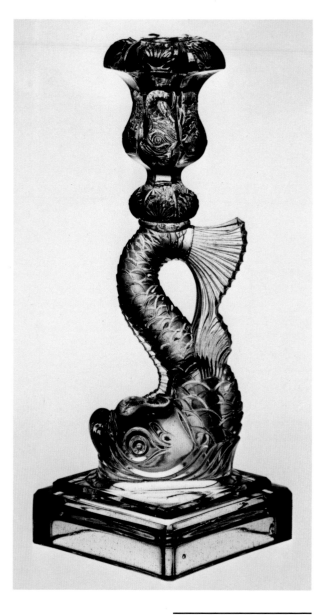

Bottle for Serving Spirits Late 18th century. Arima Factory (Finland). Height: 21.6 cm. National Museum of Finland, Helsinki

Bottles containing birds— or other such creatures— are made by fashioning the molten glass with pincers inside the vessel, after which the edges are reheated to form the mouth of the bottle. Such carafes were made in the Finnish glassworks Johannislund and Arima, which operated from 1813 to 1959. The green coloring of these bottles is due to the high iron content of the sand used in Finland.

Candlestick in the Form of a Dolphin New England, c. 1840–50. Height: 26 cm. The Corning Museum of Glass, New York

While this piece bears comparison with other figural bottles made in the United States at this time, it superficially resembles the dolphin-shaped bottle made in France; however this piece was pressed, not blown. (See opposite page).

Bottle in the Shape of a Dolphin

France, late 19th–
early 20th century. Height
(bottle and stopper):
42.8 cm, width: 15.5 cm.
Musée Municipal du Co-
gnac, France

The Legras St Denis glassworks in France specialized
in the fabrication of these
bottles, although it is not
certain whether this par-
ticular one came from their
workshops. Claude
Boucher's invention of an
apparatus for blowing hol-
low glass at the end of the
nineteenth century made
possible the production of
these objects, which were
popular advertising tools
until 1914. Liqueur man-
ufacturers used to give
these decorative bottles as
presents to their clients—
café and restaurant
owners—at year's end.

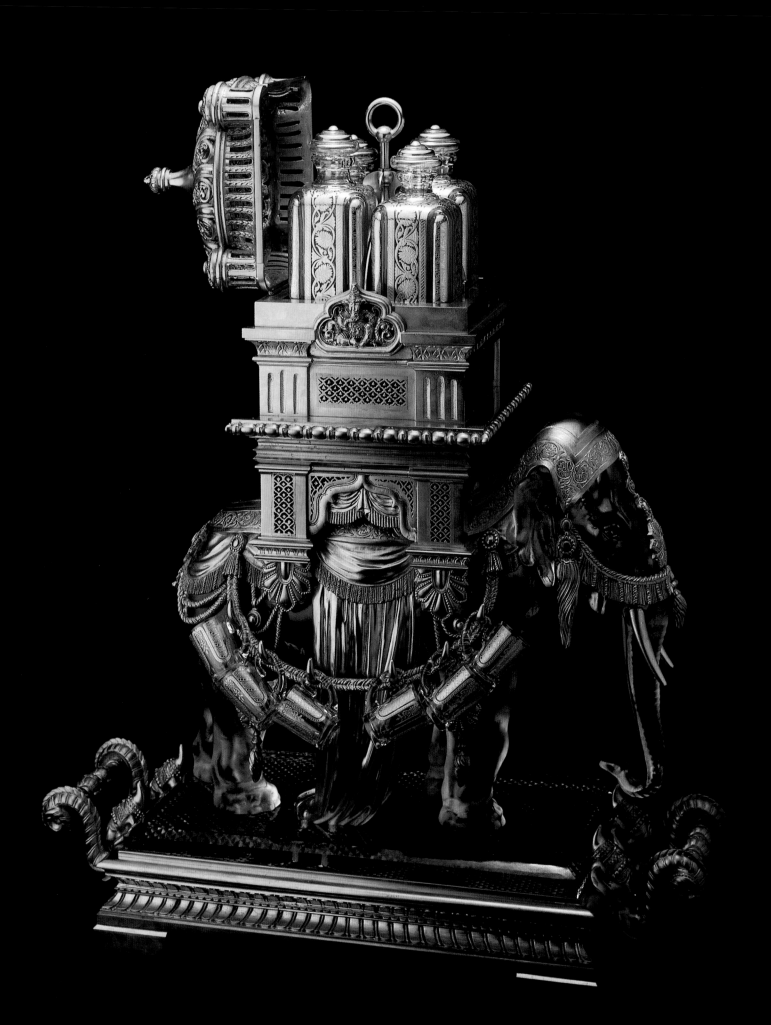

Elephant Liqueur Set
1877.
Cristallerie de Baccarat
(France). Height: 65 cm,
length: 58 cm. Musée
Baccarat, Paris

This liqueur set was en-
tered in the 1878 Paris Exposition Universelle. It
was copied from the so-
called Bastille Elephant, a
monumental bronze foun-
tain commissioned in
1808 by Napoléon Bo-
naparte to celebrate the

fourth anniversary of his
coronation. It was acquired
by the Maharajah of Bar-
oda, who purchased it to
celebrate the Indian Feast
of the Elephant. In 1984
–85 Baccarat made seven
copies of the piece.

The elephant's body is of
crystal, acid-finished and
polished. The supporting
stand has a diamond cut.
The carafes and the twelve
glasses are engraved and
gilded.

Dragonfly Dish 1904.
Cristallerie de Baccarat
(France). Length:
32.8 cm. Musée Baccarat,
Paris

In clear crystal lined with
orange-colored crystal, this
hors d'oeuvre dish is com-
pletely cut to show the
body and wings of a drag-
onfly. In 1904 the maga-
zine *Art et Décoration* held a
contest in the applied arts
for objects based on the
dragonfly.

John La Farge, like Tiffany and Healy and Millet, was a prominent designer of stained-glass windows. Influenced by Japanese art, La Farge's stained glass reveals a keen eye for pictorial representation of birds and peacocks. His regard for architecture is similarly revealed in the overall composition and structure of this window.

Vase with Butterfly Decoration 1900.
Emile Gallé (France).
Height: 24.5 cm. Courtesy Ader, Picard, Tajan.
Private collection

Just as Tiffany was renown for his favrile glass, Gallé's oeuvre was similarly bound to his achievement in *marqueterie de verres aux cristaux,* in which he created astonishing inlays of animals or flowers in vases and bottles.

Vase with Birds
1878–79.
Cristallerie de Baccarat
(France). Height: 26 cm.
Musée Baccarat, Paris

The vase is part of a group
of vases and glasses in the
Baccarat Museum. The
collection is based on subjects and drawings taken
from eighteenth- and nineteenth-century Japanese
prints, particularly by the
great painter-engraver
Hokusai. Birds and fish are
shown amid various kinds
of flora.

**Vase with Lion Decora-
tion** 1900.
Saint Louis (France).
Height: 65.1 cm, diame-
ter: 19.1 cm. Courtesy
Saint Louis, Paris

The red over clear glass
pokal is engraved in nineteenth-century Bohemian
style.

Vase 1890.
Emile Gallé (France).
Height: 15.5 cm. Private
collection. Courtesy
Sotheby's, London

Gallé's earliest hyalite or
"black" vases were shown
at the 1889 World's Fair.
The design is cut into a
layer of black glass laid
over a base of colorless
glass, which produced the
effect of mourning de-
pending on the theme se-
lected. Death was
expressed by insects, creatures of the night, or au-
tumnal references. This
vase, of a cricket and dan-
delions, is one of Gallé's
mourning vases.

Dragonfly Table Lamp
c. 1900.
Louis Comfort Tiffany
(United States). Overall
height: 45.7 cm, diameter
of shade: 40.6 cm. Cour-
tesy Christie's, New York

Unlike the more common
lamp bases typically made
in bronze, this rare example was designed with
mosaics.

**Hanging Head Dragon-
fly Table Lamp** c. 1900.
Louis Comfort Tiffany
(United States). Overall
height: 71 cm, diameter of
shade: 55.9 cm. Courtesy
Christie's, New York

The typical Tiffany lamp
was designed as a table
lamp. The base is of
bronze and the shade uses
stained glass techniques.
When diffused by a multi-
tude of small pieces of colored glass, electric light
made the piece radiate.
The delicate shape of the
dragonfly was eminently
suited to Art Nouveau
style.

Vase 1902.
Albert Dammouse for
Daum (France). Height:
4 cm, diameter: 10 cm.
Musée du Petit Palais,
Paris

A disciple of Henry Cros,
Dammouse began his ca-
reer in ceramic and por-
celain. Attempting to
obtain an effect of bril-
liance, he began to work in
pâte d'émail, halfway between ceramic and glass.
His creations in *pâte de
verre,* which he treated as
porcelain, are elegant and
luminous. Leaves and
dragonflies seem to be
floating weightlessly
against the opalescent sky-
blue background.

Perfume Bottle c. 1914.
Made for Guerlin perfume
"Champs Elysées" (France).
Height: 12.2 cm. Musée
International de la Par-
fumerie de Grasse, France

Baccarat designed a num-
ber of perfume bottles,
and this highly stylized
bottle is characteristic of
their work in which the
sculptural form of the bottle predominates.

Vase c. 1876–78.
Emile Gallé (France).
Height: 19 cm. Private
collection, France

The elegant, airy dragonfly
is the very image of Japan,
which is sometimes called
Isle of the Dragonfly. Perhaps copied directly from a
fan, the drawing and re-
spect for transparency in
this piece are not at all
what we expect from
Gallé. This was his first
contact with glass. At the
time he was following the
taste for the Asian arts that
prevailed following the
World's Fairs of 1867 and
1878, and were decor
motifs for much of Art
Nouveau.

The Fox and the Crow
1893–94.
Henri Dufour for Daum
(France). Height: 22 cm.
Daum Collection

Trained at the Faïenceries
de Lunéville in Lorraine
where he was a decorator,
Dufour brought with him
to Antonin Daum's glass-
works at Nancy the skill of
portraying scenes on por-
celain. With great finesse
and in the style of an engraving, he created
amusingly light-hearted or
moralistic little scenes in
glass. La Fontaine's
Fables—in this instance
the Fox and the Crow—
were one source of inspiration, along with the ele-
gant *scènes champêtres* so
dear to the painters of the
eighteenth century.

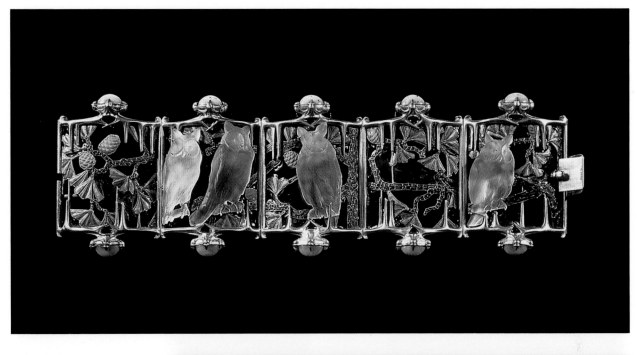

Owl Bracelet 1900–01.
René Lalique (France).
Length: 20 cm. Calouste
Gulbenkian Foundation,
Lisbon

In the nineteenth century,
jewelry design underwent
a second renaissance. The
creations of René Lalique
were enthusiastically re-
ceived by crown heads and
celebrities. Entranced by
the fantasy and opulence of
his jewels, women made
his name a byword in so-
ciety and in the world of
fashion. This bracelet is
made up of several dif-
ferent materials: chal-
cedony, enamel, and gold;
the owls are of frosted
glass.

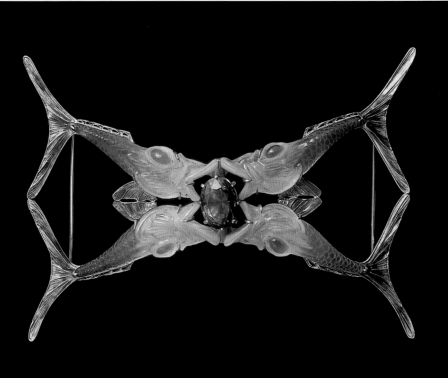

Brooch with Four Fish
c. 1900.
René Lalique (France).
Length: 11 cm. Lalique
Museum, Japan

Two facing sets of twin
fishes in blue-enameled

pâte de verre set in gold
form the setting for a sap-
phire. Lalique always
sought purity in the shapes
and subjects of his jewelry;
this brooch attests to his
love of symmetry.

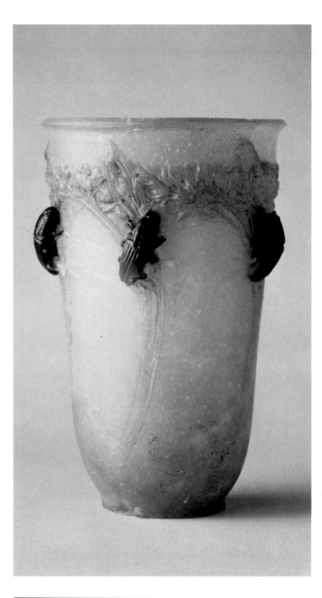

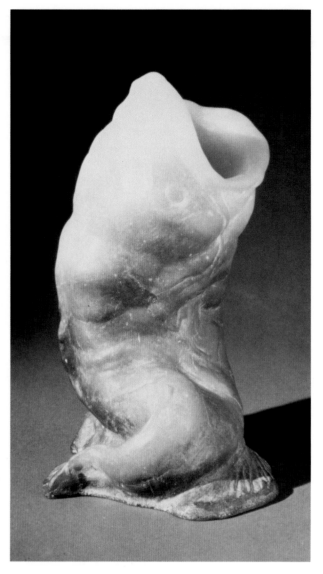

Vase with Scarab Decoration 1912.
François-Emile Décorchemont (France). Height: 17.5 cm. Musée des Arts Décoratifs, Paris

Décorchemont, a Norman painter and glassmaker, spent his entire professional life working alone in the country. Beginning in 1902, he became interested in the technical and aesthetic resources of *pâte de verre*. Décorchemont's style blossomed after 1910. His medium became more consistent, the colors more sustained. Flora, masques, scarabs, dragonflies, and fish are all shown in relief, elegantly animating the surface of the vase.

Fish c. 1900
Georges Despret (France). Height: 25.5 cm. The Corning Museum of Glass, New York

Henry Cros was responsible for developing *pâte de verre,* based on ancient glassmaking techniques, and among his disciples was Despret. In this piece Despret conveys the spirit and sensuous forms of Art Nouveau.

Ermine 1908.
Henri Bergé and Almeric Walter for Daum (France). Length: 27 cm. Daum Collection

The ermine, a carnivore with immaculate snow-white fur, symbolizes purity and innocence in justice; for this reason it is used to decorate the robes of high dignitaries and officials of State, Church, and university. It was renowned for its cruelty and its daring, as well as being sought for its fur. The *pâte de verre* example here aggressively defends its prey, a nest full of eggs, which Henri Bergé has turned into a container for jewelry.

Hippocampus 1901.
Emile Gallé (France). Height: 11.5 cm. Musée des Arts Décoratifs, Paris

Dated 1901 and dedicated to Joseph Reinach, lawyer and follower of Gambetta, the sea horse vase is Gallé's tribute to one of Dreyfus's defenders. The politician and the glassmaker were linked by many mutually held beliefs and a long correspondence. There are several examples of this gift to Reinach, which is the fruit of Gallé's last experiments.

▶

Peacock Vase 1892.
Louis Comfort Tiffany
(United States). Height:
35.9 cm, width: 29.2 cm.
The Metropolitan Museum
of Art, New York. Gift of
H. O. Havemeyer, 1896

Louis Comfort Tiffany's
work in iridescent glass
was testimony to his mas-
terful craftsmanship. The
interest in such glass was
revived in the 1870s when
a cache of ancient glass was
unearthed. Tiffany began
experimentation in the
medium, employing the
techniques of Venetian
blown glass. The result became known as favrile
glass, meaning the com-
position and amalgama-
tion of variously colored
glasses worked together
while hot. The whorls and
nuances of color possible
on favrile glass make this
peacock feather especially
sumptuous.

Amazon 1895.
Henry Cros (France). Di-
mensions: 30 × 30 cm.
Felix Marcilhac Collection,
Paris

The sculptor Henry Cros is
known for his busts, bas-
reliefs, and medallions in
wax, clay, and bronze. In
the course of his research
into ancient methods for
coloring portraits and
sculptures, Cros first
worked in encaustic, and
subsequently developed

pâte de verre. His work in
pâte de verre earned him
great respect in critical cir-
cles. He managed to have
his own workshop set up
for him, first by the Manufacture de Sèvres, and
later by the French Gov-
ernment, where he carried
on his research. For the
most part, he produced
bas-relief plaques having
Greek and Roman themes,
such as this Amazon on
horseback.

Twilight Vase 1901.
Philippe Wolfers for Val-
Saint-Lambert (Belgium).
Height: 30.5 cm. Musée
Curtius, Liège

European tradition views
the bat, another despised
creature, as either a failed
bird or a sort of winged
dragon. It haunts the night
and its frenzied flight is
like that of an evil spirit
blinded by the light. Tak-
ing up this typically Art
Nouveau theme, the gold-
smith Philippe Wolfers in-
terpreted it with great
precision. The winged
motif surrounds the vase
symmetrically and harmo-
niously. Wolfers created
the model and commis-
sioned the vase's fabrication
at the Val-Saint-Lambert
glassworks. He then en-
trusted his lapidary, Maus,
with its engraving and
cutting.

Flask with Three Wasps
1912–13.
René Lalique (France).
Height: 12 cm. Courtesy
Lalique, Paris

This piece was made during the period when Lalique was producing perfume bottles for his friend and renowned perfumer, Coty. Its graphic design is a precursor of Art Deco.

Christmas Tree Ornament in the Shape of a Dog
United States, 20th century. Height: 11.4 cm, width: 5.1 cm. The Brooklyn Museum (82.112.4). Gift of Fred Tannery

No Christmas tree is worthy of the name unless it is decorated with an abundance of ornaments and figurines. This mold-blown glass dog, seated with its right paw to its ear, is an amusing example. On the head, covered in glittering crystals, is a cap with a ring for hanging from the tree. Most Christmas tree ornaments and lights were made in Germany and Bohemia, now Czechoslovakia.

Lamp with Owl Decoration c. 1900.
Antonin Daum for Daum (France). Height: 85 cm.
Daum Collection

Created for Antonin Daum's desk, this owl shed a luminous glow over his creative activities.

Dragonfly Bowl 1904.
Emile Gallé (France).
Height: 14.5 cm. Private
collection. Courtesy Christie's, Geneva

The insect most often present in Gallé's work, the

dragonfly ends the series of
work in animals and in-
sects. Having gone beyond
the inspiration originally
from the Japanese, the
dragonfly exemplifies
Gallé's technique and
craftsmanship.

Vase with Antlered Moose
Bohemia, 1st quarter of 19th century. Height: 12.5 cm. Courtesy Glassgallery Michael Kovacek, Vienna

An exquisite example of glass engraving is this colorless vase with a twelve-point star-cut base. The overall scene could be likened to a pastoral setting, what with the beauty of the great stag leaping effortlessly over the hound, in pursuit at its heels. The hunting horn and bag for game shown in the polished panel was reserved for a personal dedication that the owner might wish to have engraved.

Wineglass with Horse Decoration 1876. Saint-Louis (France). Height: 21 cm. Courtesy Saint-Louis, Paris

Table services were the basis of the production of the Saint-Louis glassworks. Stag-hunting was common in that region of eastern France, and the horse stands nobly engraved on the crystal.

GLASS IN THE MODERN AGE: 1915-1976

In the sixty years covered here, glassmaking evolved through a series of artistic styles and was affected by technical discoveries yielding new clarity, lower melting temperatures, and more options for forming and decorating.

The First World War disrupted the glass industry both in America (where materials and fuel were scarce) and in Europe, except for the neutral Scandinavian countries. During the war years, Swedish makers concentrated on applying good design to mass-produced wares. At Orrefors, designers Simon Gate and Edward Hald introduced *graal* glass, which encased relief-cut designs in a layer of clear crystal. With their headstart, the Scandinavian makers emerged as a strong force in glass production in the 1920s, creating colorless crystal wares that often were decoratively copper-wheel engraved with classic designs. About 1930, Orrefors pioneered the *ariel* glass technique of encasing sandblasted layers of glass, along with trapped air, in clear and colored crystal.

French glassmakers, meanwhile, abandoned the sinuous decorative lines of Art Nouveau for the newer Art Deco aesthetic. Named for the Exposition Internationale des Arts Décoratifs et Industriels Modernes held in Paris in 1925, Art Deco rejected things that were merely pretty; forms were celebrated for their stylized, linear, and geometric outlines. Much in the way that Cubist painters distorted the lines of their subjects, glassmakers like Aristide Colotte and René Lalique used molding, acid-etching, and other techniques to fracture the surface of glass vessels, producing dramatic geometric forms.

During the 1920s, Lalique emerged as the most versatile French glasshouse, offering a wide range of mass-produced pressed and blown wares including vases, sculptural figures, and all manner of useful objects, including clocks (page 137) in the Art Deco mode. Daum, too, created sculptural figures in the Art Deco aesthetic during this decade.

The Frenchmen Almeric Walter, François-Emile Décorchement, and

Vase 1925.
Emile Wirtz for Daum (France). Blown glass with acid technique. Height: 25.7 cm. Daum Collection

Gabriel Argy-Rousseau continued their work with *pâte de verre* during the 20s and 30s. Perhaps the most forward-looking of the French glassmakers, however, was Maurice Marinot, an established Fauvist who took an interest in enameling glass around 1911. By 1922, Marinot was manipulating the glass itself in a sculptural way, turning out thick-walled vessels of clear crystal, deeply cut or acid-etched, sometimes enclosing trapped air (page 144). Another atypical French glass artist, the expatriate Catalonian Jean Sala, formed birds and fishes of rough-textured, free-blown glass (page 174).

Except in Italy, the popularity of colored glass declined after 1930, while cut and etched wares of clear crystal enjoyed a greater vogue. By 1933, Steuben Glass had turned away from the colored glass it had produced since 1903 under the direction of Frederick Carder. Led by Arthur A. Houghton, Jr., the company began offering a new line of colorless, highly refractive, blown and wheel-engraved crystal exemplified by Sidney Waugh's Orrefors-influenced *Gazelle Bowl* (page 147). In the late 30s, Steuben invited twenty-seven artists of international reputation, including Isamu Noguchi (page 146), Georgia O'Keeffe, and Aristide Maillol to create designs to be engraved on a series of Steuben bowls and plates. This signalled the start of Steuben's continuing effort to involve artists in the production of glass.

By the mid-1930s, Modernism had emerged as the dominant aesthetic. This movement eschewed decoration and embraced purity of line and form and "truth in materials" (which meant, for glassmakers, using blown techniques that emphasized the ductility of the glass). Architects and craftsmen who trained at the Bauhaus under Walter Gropius and Mies van der Rohe spread the movement worldwide so that, in the years preceding World War II, it truly became an "International Style." The look was popularized by the 1939 New York World's Fair, which offered a showcase for the colorless, simply blown and engraved wares of Steuben, Baccarat, and other glasshouses.

World War II devastated the European glassmaking centers, except for those in neutral Sweden; Daum and many other companies ceased production for several years. When they reopened in the late 1940s and early 1950s, the emphasis was less on artistic glass than on utilitarian tablewares and small blown or pressed figures. But as prosperity returned, it brought with it a reordering of society and a certain democratization of culture that created new markets for ornamental glass in both Europe and America. By the 1950s, Steuben, Baccarat, Daum, and Lalique were producing molded or blown birds, deer, and other creatures in crystal. A generation of glass animal collectors had emerged, and their demands fueled the production of glass animal figures for the next few decades. So great was this interest that in 1971,

Steuben arranged "The Animal Fair," an exhibition of sixty glass animals, at its New York City gallery.

Other postwar trends included the return of colored glass, especially at the Murano glasshouses of Venini and Vetri d'Arte, which continued to employ traditional Venetian blowing and lampworking techniques in the creation of modern free-form pieces and animal figures (page 132).

But the most important development of the postwar decades was the rise of the Studio Movement in glassmaking. For the first time, individuals working in home studios were able to both design and fabricate artistic glasswares. Previously, throughout the first half of the twentieth century, artistic glass had invariably been designed in the "studio departments" attached to many major factories and operated more for prestige than profit. With few exceptions, the people who designed these artistic wares were not the ones who produced them; a team approach involving both glass designer and craftsman was the norm at Orrefors, Steuben, and elsewhere. At "Glass 1959," an open juried exhibition sponsored by the Corning Museum of Glass, most of the wares shown were utilitarian, and about ninety percent had been entered by glass-making factories rather than individuals.

Spurred by the example of artist/craftsmen in Czechoslovakia and Sweden, however, the interest in using glass as a medium for individual artistic expression grew. The Americans Harvey Littleton and Dominick Labino are credited with pioneering this trend at a glassmaking workshop held at the Toledo (Ohio) Museum of Art in 1962. Littleton was the ceramic designer of the pair; Labino the technician who invented a special glass formula with a relatively low melting point, and fashioned a small furnace suitable for individual use in home studios and classrooms. For the first time, using Labino's formula and furnace, it became possible for craftsmen to create artistic glass independent of the factory environment.

The Studio Movement spread quickly in the United States. By the mid-1970s, some 100 craft schools, colleges, and universities were offering instruction in glassmaking, and publications dealing with glass were proliferating. While trade fairs (especially the Milan Triennale of 1957 and 1960 and the fairs at Belgium in 1958, Brazil in 1965, Mexico in 1966, and Canada in 1967) served as showcases for glass factories, museum exhibitions took on new importance as a stimulus to individual studio glassmakers.

By 1976, the Studio Movement was well established not only in America, but in Sweden, Czechoslovakia, England, Germany, Finland, and elsewhere. Following in the footsteps of Marinot, studio glassmakers now considered glass primarily as a medium for creativity, unfettered by utilitarian concerns.

THE MENAGERIE OF THE BACCARAT MUSEUM IN PARIS

Baccarat was founded in 1764 by Louis XV at the request of the Bishop of Metz, Louis de Montmorency-Laval, to relieve unemployment and stop the outflow of French cash for the purchase of Bohemian glass, highly fashionable at that time. The glassworks was established on the Meurthe River, across from the ancient town of Baccarat.

Baccarat's best period was from 1822 to 1858, when it produced crystal tableware, decorative vases, opaline glass, and the *millefiori* paperweights then greatly in vogue. During the nineteenth century, almost every royal family commissioned works from this factory. It was the custom to make two of every object commissioned, one example to be kept by the factory. In this way, Baccarat started its own collection, which is now housed in the Baccarat Museum at 30 bis rue de Paradis, Paris. A public showcase, the museum enables visitors to review the development of Baccarat's technique and style over the years.

The glassworks at Baccarat continued to produce luxury items throughout the nineteenth century and up to the present time, always keeping abreast of industry changes in style and technique. Baccarat invariably showed its finest wares at the various World's Fairs and industrial expositions that took place over the years. Recently, the firm recreated a limited number of reproductions of an Elephant Cellarette displayed at the Paris Exposition of 1878. Twenty-three other pieces in the Museum's collection, typifying the development of Baccarat were also reproduced in 1986.

In addition to its nineteenth-century glass, the Baccarat Museum serves as a showcase for the creations of twentieth-century designers including Georges Chevalier, who contributed a series of crystal animals in the 1950s and 1960s. Artists commissioned by Baccarat to make animal-related glass designs include American sculptor and painter Tauni de Lesseps, American ceramist Katherine de Sousa, and the Surrealist painter Salvador Dalí.

All together, the many animal figures and images created by these and other artists in Baccarat glass amount to a veritable menagerie. In this zoo are many familiar animals: the duck (Bureau d'Études Baccarat, 1950 and 1957), the rabbit (Georges Chevalier, 1960), and the horse (Bernard Augst, 1964, and Tauni de Lesseps, 1977). There are birds, like Robert Rigot's screech-owls from 1968 and 1972, plus falcons, kingfishers, and hoot-owls by various designers. There are fish and wild beasts, including Georges Chevalier's favorite polar bear, Egyptian cat, elephant (1962), and giraffe (1963).

For the animal lover, a visit to this timeless bestiary is always a delight.

Gridel Paperweight with White Squirrel 1972.
Cristallerie de Baccarat (France). Lead crystal. Diameter: 7.9 cm. Musée Baccarat, Paris

Squirrel 1962.
Georges Chevalier for Cristallerie de Baccarat (France). Lead crystal. Height: 11 cm. Cristallerie de Baccarat, Paris

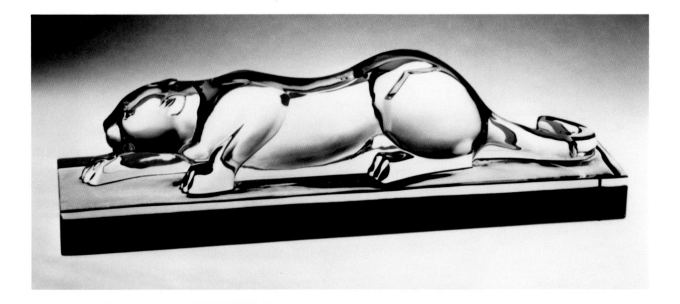

Panther 1937.
Bureau d'Études Baccarat
(France). Recut crystal.
Length: 51 cm. The Corning Museum of Glass,
New York

Duck 1950.
Cristallerie de Baccarat
(France). Clear crystal,
molded and recut. Height:
21.5 cm. Cristallerie de
Baccarat, Paris

Stag's Head 1949.
Georges Chevalier for
Cristallerie de Baccarat
(France). Lead crystal.
Height: 41 cm. Musée
Baccarat, Paris

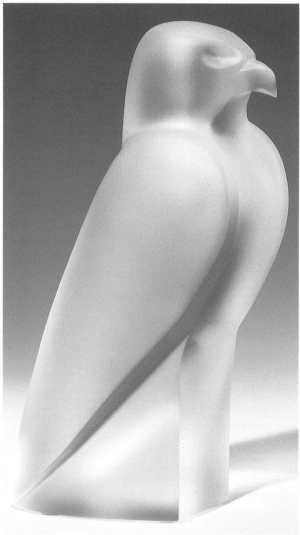

Falcon 1968.
Cristallerie de Baccarat
(France). Lead crystal.
Height: 26 cm.
Cristallerie de Baccarat,
Paris

Swan 1924.
Georges Chevalier for
Cristallerie de Baccarat
(France). Clear crystal,
pressed and cut. Height:
20 cm. Musée Baccarat,
Paris

DAUM: CRISTALLERIE DE NANCY

The Daum glass firm has been located in Nancy since about 1870, when Jean Daum founded it to produce window glass. That business failed to prosper, and upon Jean Daum's death in 1885, the brothers Auguste (1853–1909) and Antonin (1864–1930) Daum set about to change its direction.

From 1889 to 1914, they used the techniques of enameling, acid-etching, and cameo-cutting to produce decorative wares in the Art Nouveau mode pioneered by neighboring Nancy glassmaker Emile Gallé. Inspired by the beauty of the Lorraine landscape, the brothers Daum developed new methods to depict its flora and fauna in glass. At the Paris Exhibition of 1900, they won a prize for their intercalary technique, in which vessels were built up from several layers of cameo-cut glass interspersed with clear crystal casing for an effect of great depth and naturalism.

Antonin Daum admired the decorative possibilities of *pâte de verre,* and in 1906 he hired Almeric Walter from the Sèvres ceramic school to develop such a line. Working as a team with glass technician Henri Bergé, Walter created a notable group of small *pâte de verre* sculptures of animals and women before leaving Daum to set up his own business.

The factory closed during World War I, reopening in 1919 under the direction of Paul Daum. During the 1920s, cameo-cut vases in the Art Deco style were a staple. In later decades, the firm turned to pressed and molded wares of clear crystal, including, in the 1960s and 70s, a collection of animal figures that were largely the work of staff designers.

In 1968, Daum revived the process of working in *pâte de verre,* commissioning Salvador Dalí to produce a limited-edition plaque of a winged horse. Under the direction of Michael Daum, other distinguished designers—Claude Lhoste, Dan Dailey, and Peter Yenawine among them—have also been engaged to create *pâte de verre* animals.

Waterbirds 1967.
Daum, Cristallerie de
Nancy (France). Crystal.
Height: 23 cm. Courtesy
Daum, Paris

Sparrows 1967.
Daum, Cristallerie de
Nancy (France). Crystal.
Height: 6.5 cm. Courtesy
Daum, Paris

Chinese Fish 1957. Daum, Cristallerie de Nancy (France). Crystal. Height: 30 cm. Courtesy Daum, Paris

Buffalo 1969. Daum, Cristallerie de Nancy (France). Crystal. Length: 27.9 cm. Courtesy Daum, Paris

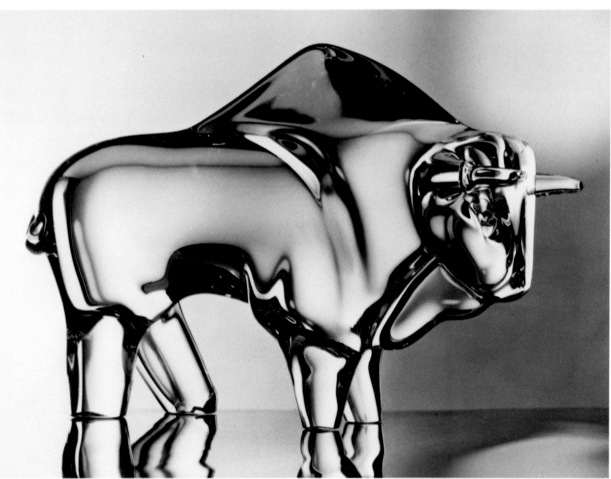

Pegasus 1968.
Salvador Dalí for Daum,
Cristallerie de Nancy
(France). *Pâte de verre.*
Height: 36 cm, width:
33 cm. Daum, Cristallerie
de Nancy

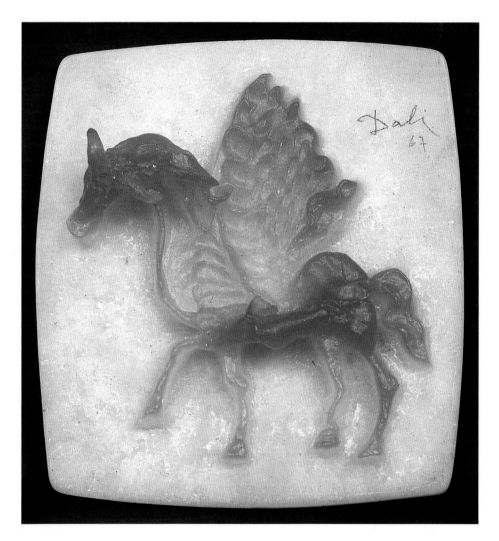

Hidden Peace 1975.
Pedro Ramirez Vazquez for
Daum, Cristallerie de
Nancy (France). *Pâte de
verre.* Length: 26 cm.
Courtesy Daum, Paris

Rabbit 1968.
Daum, Cristallerie de
Nancy (France). Crystal.
Length: 13 cm. Courtesy
Daum, Paris

Teddy bear 1969.
Daum, Cristallerie de
Nancy (France). Crystal.
Height: 17 cm. Courtesy
Daum, Paris

Horse 1975.
Daum, Cristallerie de
Nancy (France). Crystal.
Height: 35 cm. Courtesy
Daum, Paris

Tiger 1974.
Daum, Cristallerie de
Nancy (France). Crystal.
Length: 50 cm. Courtesy
Daum, Paris

Cats 1968.
Daum, Cristallerie de
Nancy (France). Crystal.
Height: 25 cm. Courtesy
Daum, Paris

Italian Glassmakers:
Venini, Barovier, Seguso

Just as the island of Murano has dominated the Italian glass industry for 700 years, so most of the well-known names in Italian glass today are those of centuries-old families. Barovier, for example, has had illustrious associations with glassmaking since the fifteenth century, when Angelo Barovier produced *lattimo*—the white milk glass that, drawn out into threads, forms the basis for the *latticinio* technique still favored by contemporary Italian artisans.

In 1878, Angelo Barovier's descendants set up their own Murano factory, Fratelli Barovier, to produce glass in classic sixteenth-century Venetian styles. The firm became Barovier Toso in 1936 and, under the direction of Ercole Barovier, turned out vessels in simple, flowing, modern styles, as well as animal figures decorated in the *filigree* technique.

Another 1920s innovator who revived the fifteenth-century techniques of the Venetian glassmakers and applied them to modern forms was Paoli Venini, a lawyer turned glassmaker. He became a partner in Giacomo Cappelinis Murano glasshouse in 1921, then took over and renamed the firm Venini and Company in 1925. Since that time, the Venini glasshouse has been a strong force in Italian glass design.

Closed down during the war, Venini distinguished itself in the postwar decades with a series of designs by architect Gio Ponti. During the 1950s, Venini glass was known for its bright primary colors—a trend that spread to other Italian firms and that continues today. Venini has produced animal figures touched with characteristic primary hues.

A third prominent Murano firm, Seguso Vetri d'Arte, employed designer Flavio Poli to create massive sculptural vases as well as whimsical bird and animal forms using traditional techniques.

The old-fashioned craft tradition persists in Murano, where off-hand forming and lampworking techniques still dominate the industry. Virtually all contemporary Murano glass—including many whimsical animal figures—is both shaped and decorated at the lamp or furnace, to the exclusion of engraving and other cold-working techniques. And the Murano houses are still known for their use of exuberant color.

Tradition in craftsmanship and method, fantasy and charm in concept—these have always been, and they remain, Murano's great achievements in animal art as in other forms of glass.

Fish 1961.
Ken Scott for Venini (Italy). Opaline glass with threads of color. Length: 12–30 cm. Courtesy Venini, Italy

Pigeon 1963.
Venini (Italy). Colored iridescent glass. Length: 20 cm. Francesco Coccia Collection

Tiger c. 1928.
Ercole Barovier (Venice).
Blown glass, applied glass
on head, legs, and tail,
gold finish. Height:
15.2 cm, length: 33.0 cm.
Courtesy Muriel Karasik
Gallery, New York

Vase (from the Barbarico series) 1951.
Ercole Barovier (Italy).
Black glass, blown.
Height: 15 cm. Musée des
Arts Décoratifs, Paris

Goose c. 1950.
Designed by Flavio Poli
and crafted by Archimede
Seguso for Seguso Vetri
d'Arte (Italy). Green, non-
lead glass. Height: 27 cm.
The Corning Museum of
Glass, New York

Fox Hood Ornament
1931.
René Lalique (France). Satin glass figure on radiator
cap. Length: 15 cm. Cour-
tesy Lalique, Paris

**Black & White Collec-
tion** c. 1960.
Archimede Seguso (Italy).
Black and opaque white
glass. Bear: 39 cm, paperweights: 8, 7, and 6 cm,
seal: 19 cm. Private
collection

LALIQUE: A GLASSMAKING FAMILY

Three generations of Laliques have been closely bound up in the evolution of the family business: René Lalique, Marc Lalique, and Marie-Claude Lalique.

The firm began in 1885 as a jewelry workshop in Paris. There, René Lalique experimented with glass, combining it with gold and semiprecious stones in a series of remarkable pendants, combs, and brooches with stylized Art Nouveau figures: dragonflies, bats, female figures, and flowers. These he sold through Samuel Bing's L'Art Nouveau shop, and he exhibited many of them to great acclaim at the Paris Exhibition of 1900.

In 1908, having received a commission from his friend François Coty to produce perfume bottles, Lalique purchased a small glasshouse at Combes-La-Ville, where he turned out both blown and molded wares. At the close of the First World War, he built a larger factory in Alsace, at Wingen-sur-Moder. There, Lalique designed and produced a wide range of mechanically molded and pressed vases, stem- and tablewares mainly in colorless or pale-hued transparent crystal, sometimes with contrasting opaque black glass decoration. Lalique also specialized in the sculptural figures of women and animals, some cast using the "lost wax" method.

The firm was closely attuned to stylistic change; by the early 1920s, their crystal exhibited the hard linear designs of the Art Deco mode, yet retained the detailed, flowing surface textures that set apart René Lalique's glass. Soon,

Lalique became France's foremost producer of household, architectural, and ornamental glass. Their wares drew praise at the Exposition Internationale des Arts Décoratifs et Industriels Modernes in Paris in 1925.

Lalique ceased production during World War I, and René died in 1945. When the firm reopened, it was under the artistic direction and management of his son, Marc. Soon Lalique was back on its pre-war footing, showing a wide range of glass at the government-sponsored "L'Art du Verre" exhibition at the Louvre in 1951.

Marc Lalique's postwar designs tended to be geometric rather than figural, with the exception of a series of crystal animals: roosters, deer, and turtledoves. His glass employed color—usually blue—sparingly; it could be transparent or finished with acid for a misty effect.

Marie-Claude Lalique, third in succession, inherited her grandfather's bent toward the experimental. Fascinated by jewelry, she has played with enamels and semiprecious stones, acquiring a taste for color that is apparent in her opaline glass wares. Her animal figures in particular are produced in yellow, amber, pale blue, and green opaline.

Faithful to tradition, she has regularly added new animals to the Lalique bestiary. Her passion for cats is especially apparent, and her travels have inspired such pieces as the head of a sacred ram and a flock of swallows fleeing the cold. Thus Lalique's creativity continues.

Lamp 1925.
René Lalique (France).
Molded and wheel-cut
decoration on a bakelite
base. Height: 45.1 cm.
Victoria and Albert Mu-
seum, London. Handley
Read Collection

Formose c. 1920–30.
René Lalique (France).
Colored glass. Height:
17 cm, diameter:
17.3 cm. Kunstmuseum,
Düsseldorf, Germany

Centerpiece Yeso 1922.
René Lalique (France).
Sculpture of clear glass, satin, molded. Height:
33.5 cm. Courtesy La-
lique, Paris

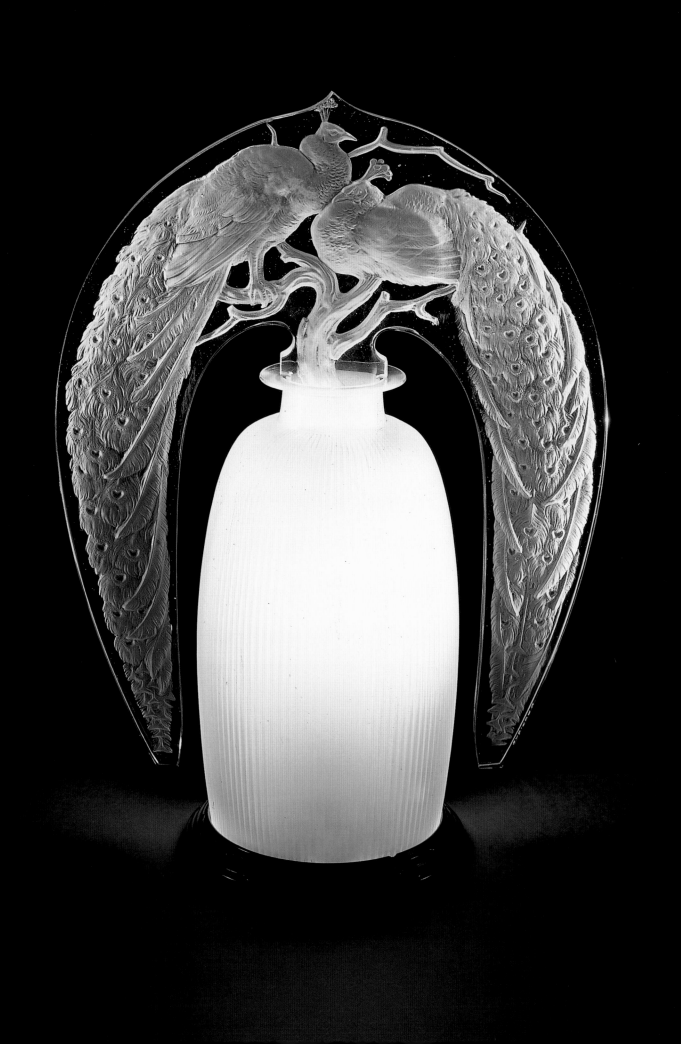

Vase with Grasshopper Decoration 1924.
René Lalique (France).
Clear patinated glass vase, with blue-gray enameling.
Height: 28 cm. Private collection. Courtesy Sotheby's, London

Snake Vase 1925.
René Lalique (France).
Colored glass. Height: 26 cm. Courtesy Lalique, Paris

Wild Boar 1929.
René Lalique (France). Satin finish. Length:
9.3 cm. Courtesy Lalique,
Paris

Small Clock with Swallows 1926–27.
René Lalique (France).
Clock encased in clear
glass frame, enameled
swallows. Height: 15 cm.
Courtesy Lalique, Paris

Mask 1928.
René Lalique (France). Satin crystal. Height:
31 cm. Courtesy Lalique,
Paris

Lamp with Ram Motif
1931.
René Lalique (France).
Transparent glass, satin.
Height: 24 cm. Courtesy
Lalique, Paris

Lamp with Cicada Motif
1931.
René Lalique (France).
Transparent glass, satin.
Height: 24 cm. Courtesy
Lalique, Paris

Macaw 1951.
Marc Lalique for Cristal Lalique (France). Satin crystal figure. Height: 29.5 cm. Cristal Lalique, Paris

Turtledoves 1954.
Marc Lalique for Cristal Lalique (France). Clear and satin crystal with colored highlights. Height: 20.0–21.0 cm. Courtesy Lalique, Paris

Stag Console 1947.
Marc Lalique for Cristal
Lalique (France). Satin
crystal. Height: 29 cm.
Cristal Lalique, Paris

Rooster 1953.
Marc Lalique for Cristal
Lalique (France). Clear
crystal. Height: 45 cm.
Cristal Lalique, Paris

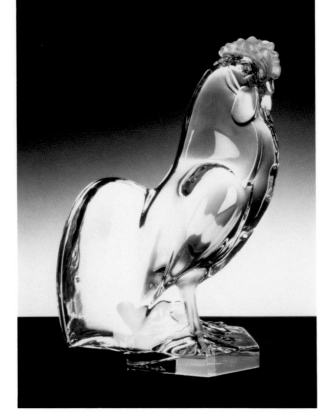

"Pilmico" Birds 1955. Marc Lalique for Cristal Lalique (France). Clear satin crystal and blue colored crystal. Height: 12 cm. Cristal Lalique, Paris

Deer 1958. Marc Lalique for Cristal Lalique (France). Satin crystal. Height: 25.5 cm. Cristal Lalique, Paris

Louisiana Ibis 1975. Marc Lalique for Cristal Lalique (France). Satin crystal, engraved. Height: 35.5 cm. Cristal Lalique, Paris

Hedgehog "Valentin" 1974. Marie-Claude Lalique for Cristal Lalique (France). Satin crystal, engraved. Length: 13 cm. Cristal Lalique, Paris

Large Flask 1922.
Maurice Marinot (France).
Engraved glass with two
colors, absinthe green and
white. Height: 25 cm.
Francis Briest Collection,
Paris

MAURICE MARINOT: PAINTER AND GLASSMAKER

Maurice Marinot (1882–1960) was a pioneer: the first artist to learn the glassmaker's craft and make it the medium for passionate artistic expression. Born at Troyes and educated at L'École des Beaux Arts in Paris, he worked briefly in the studio of Fernand Cormon. Marinot exhibited his canvases regularly in Paris until 1913 where his bold palette earned him a place among the Fauve painters.

In 1911, on a visit to the Bar-sur-Seine glasshouse of his friends Eugène and Gabriel Viard, the painter Marinot became intrigued with the idea of using glass as a canvas. For the next decade, he worked at Bar-sur-Seine, painting glass vessels with characteristic bright enamels. Gradually, he mastered the entire craft of glassmaking, in which he saw

reflected the elemental forces of nature: fire, water, ice.

By 1922, Marinot was ready to leave enameling behind. Glass for him was no longer a canvas but the sculptural medium in which to express his artistic passion. He used the techniques of acid-etching, cutting, and air-trapping to create unique effects in brilliantly textured, thick-walled vases and vessels of clear crystal.

Marinot spent long days at the furnace, followed by evenings given to design, study, and planning. Devoted as he was to the art of glass, ill health forced him to give up glassblowing in 1937, and he returned to painting. His legacy, however, remains an inspiration to artists in glass.

Steuben's Crystal Ark

For more than eighty years, Steuben crystal has been made by hand in Corning, New York, using the traditional glassmaker's tools and following methods of blowing and engraving that are centuries old.

But Steuben did not always produce the colorless, brilliantly refractive glass for which it is known today. From 1903, when the company was founded by English glassmaker Frederick Carder, to 1933, when it was reorganized under the ownership of Corning Glass and the presidency of Arthur Houghton, the mainstay of Steuben's production was a vast array of colorful art glass.

Houghton perceived that taste had shifted away from colored wares. With the help of young architect John Monteith Gates and sculptor Sidney Waugh, Houghton developed a new Steuben aesthetic, discontinuing colored glass and introducing a line of brilliant clear crystal based on a highly refractive new glass formula recently discovered at Corning.

Then, as now, many of the most striking pieces of Steuben glass were planned by designers working both in the company's New York City and Corning studios, and produced by talented glassblowers and wheel-engravers at the upstate factory in Corning.

In the fifty years since Steuben gave up colored glass, animals have comprised an important part of the company's oeuvre. They range from a decorative cat engraving designed by Isamu Noguchi for a plate in the 1940 "Twenty-Seven Artists in Crystal" series to staff designer Donald Pollard's stylized owls of 1955. Each of the technical and artistic innovations that characterized Steuben's postwar history—asymmetrical shearing, the use of precious metals in combination with glass, shapes achieved by sag-molding or pressing, among others,—has been documented in animal form.

For example, when Steuben revived the century-old process of hand pressing in its Corning factory in the late 1970s, it was used to produce a series of small, rounded animal forms known collectively as "hand coolers."

There is scarcely a creature that walks or crawls, swims or flies, that has not been captured in Steuben's sparkling crystal, representing a half-century of creativity in American glassmaking.

Frog Prince 1973.
Lloyd Atkins for Steuben
Glass (United States).
Crystal frog with gold
crown. Height: 15.2 cm.
Steuben Glass, New York

Gazelle Bowl 1935.
Sidney Waugh for Steuben
Glass (United States).
Heavy bowl blown of clear
crystal, resting on a solid
crystal base cut into four
flanges. The bowl is cop-
per-wheel engraved. Di-
ameter: 16.5 cm. Steuben
Glass, New York

**Candy Dish with Ram's
Head Finial** 1943.
Irene Benton for Steuben
Glass (United States). Cov-
ered crystal candy dish.
Height: 12.7 cm. Steuben
Glass, New York

The Cat 1940.
Isamu Noguchi for
Steuben Glass (United
States). Engraved glass.
Diameter: 25.1 cm. Co-
lumbus Museum of Art,
Ohio. Gift of Sallie Jones
Sexton in memory of her
parents, Mr. & Mrs. John
Sutphin Jones

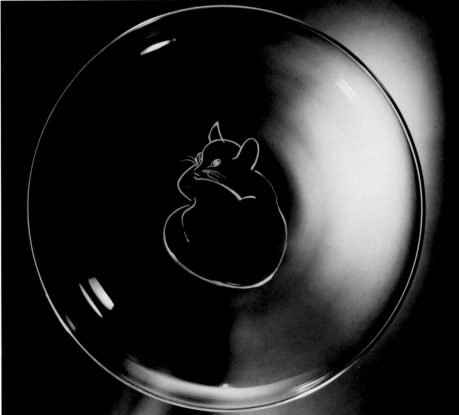

Puma Killing Snake
1941.
Frederick Carder (United States). Clear lead glass. Length: 20 cm. The Corning Museum of Glass, New York. Gift of Corning Glass Works

Whale 1956.
Lloyd Atkins for Steuben Glass (United States). Crystal. Length: 12.1 cm, height: 12.7 cm. Steuben Glass, New York

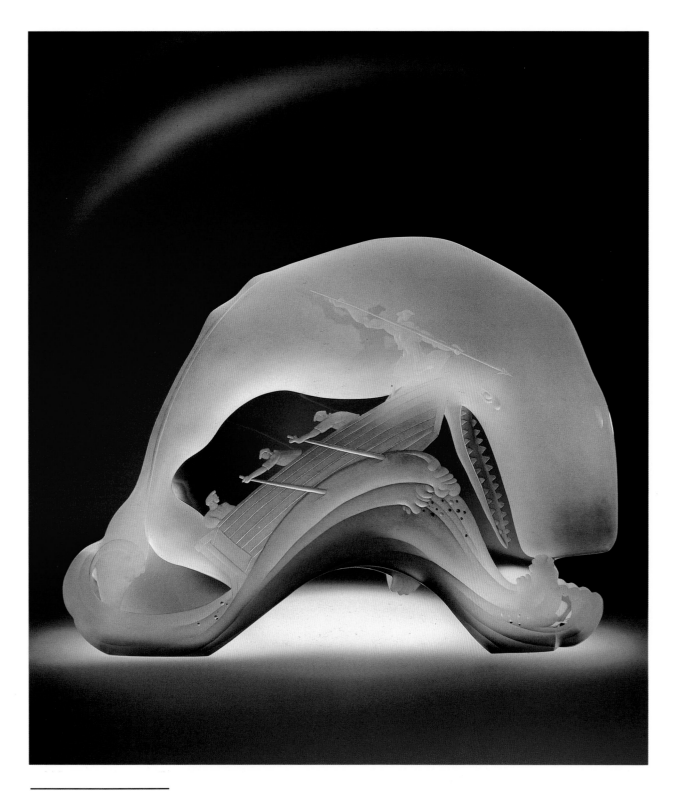

Moby Dick 1959.
Donald Pollard (glass design) and Sidney Waugh
(engraving design) for
Steuben Glass (United
States). Crystal. Length:
28.6 cm. Steuben Glass,
New York

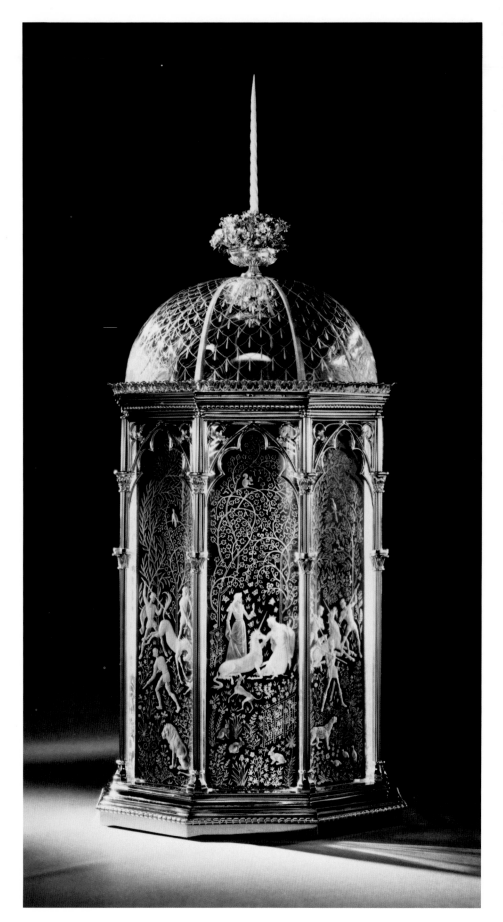

The Unicorn and the Maiden 1950. Donald Pollard (glass design) and Alexander Seidel (engraving design) for Steuben Glass (United States). Octagonal temple of crystal and gold. Height: 36.8 cm, width: 15.9 cm. Steuben Glass, New York

Trout and Fly 1966.
James Houston for Steuben
Glass (United States).
Crystal trout; 18-karat
gold fly. Height: 24.1 cm.
Steuben Glass, New York

Eagle 1964.
James Houston for Steuben
Glass (United States).
Crystal eagle on a crystal
globe. Wingspread:
30.5 cm. Steuben Glass,
New York

The Butterfly 1967.
George Thompson (glass
design) and Alexander
Seidel (engraving design)
for Steuben Glass (United
States). Crystal prism with
engraved butterfly.
Height: 20.3 cm, width:
16.5 cm. Steuben Glass,
New York

The Unicorn 1962.
George Thompson (glass
design) and Sheik Ahmed
(engraving design) for
Steuben Glass (United
States). Crystal plaque en-
graved. Height: 22.2 cm.
Steuben Glass, New York

**Beavers with Garnet
Eyes** 1975.
Lloyd Atkins for Steuben
Glass (United States). Pair
of hand-formed crystal
beavers. Upright beaver,
height: 15.9 cm. Sitting
beaver, length: 23.5 cm.
Steuben Glass, New York

Baby Koala 1971.
Lloyd Atkins for Steuben
Glass (United States).
Crystal. Height: 14.6 cm.
Steuben Glass, New York

Sea Chase 1969.
Lloyd Atkins for Steuben
Glass (United States).
Crystal glass. Height,
with base: 27.3 cm, width
of base: 43.2 cm. Steuben
Glass, New York

Flying Eagle 1975.
Paul Schulze for Steuben
Glass (United States). Flying eagle of blown crystal
with solid cut crystal head
and engraved eyes, all
formed by hand from a
single gather. Length:
36.8 cm, width: 31.8 cm,
height: 26 cm. Steuben
Glass, New York

American Eagle 1975.
Donald Pollard for Steuben
Glass (United States). Bald
eagle made of solid crys-
tal—molded, polished,
and cut. Length: 14 cm,
height: 12.1 cm. Steuben
Glass, New York

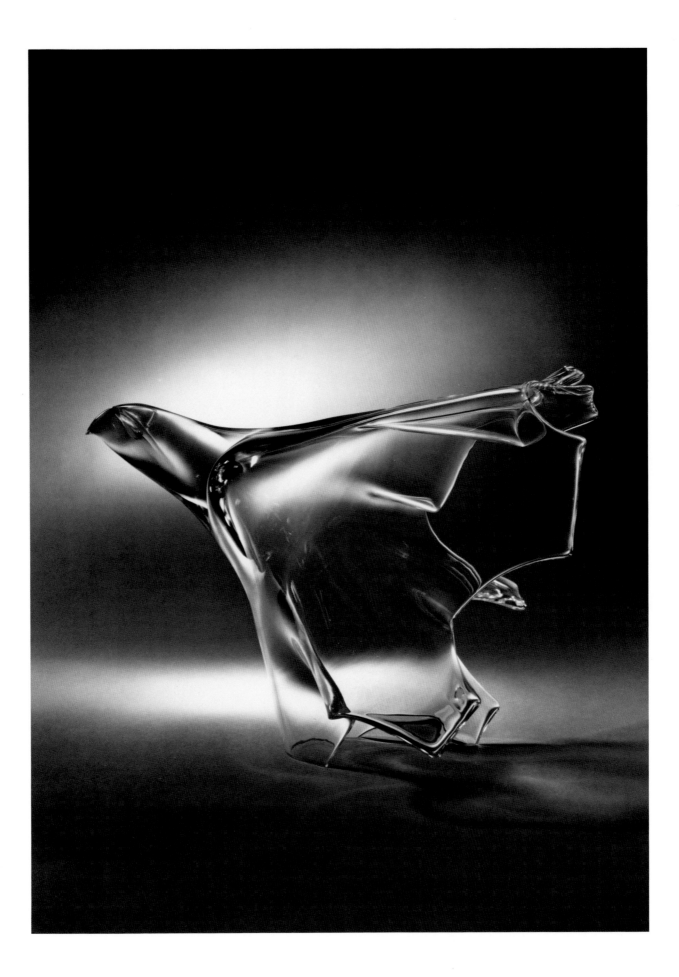

SWEDISH GLASSHOUSES: ORREFORS AND KOSTA

Since 1742, when the Kosta glassworks was established, the forested Småland lowlands of southern Sweden have been "home" to the Swedish glassmaking industry. As the impact of the Studio Glass Movement was felt in Småland in the late 1960s and 70s, glass artists began to work outside the older factories in small studios, assisted by master glass craftsmen.

It was also at Småland in 1726 that the Orrefors company began business as an iron foundry. In the 1890s, the firm reorganized to make bottles and simple domestic glass, and by 1914, under the ownership of John Ekman, it began to manufacture a new range of decorative wares. During World War I, Ekman and factory manager Albert Ahlin hired Simon Gate and Edward Hald—both trained as painters—to design glass.

Gate, Hald, and master glassblower Knut Bergqvist formed a studio team responsible for developing two of the twentieth century's most remarkable glassmaking techniques: *graal* and *ariel*. In making *graal* glass, a vessel with relief-cut surface decoration is encased in a layer of clear crystal. With the *ariel* technique, developed around 1930 and still popular, the glass object is sandblasted, creating pits and grooves that trap air when the final clear casing is applied. In the 1920s, Orrefors also made finely engraved, colorless lead crystal wares, leading the industry away from colored glass and in an entirely new direction.

But Orrefors's greatest contribution was perhaps the studio concept of teaming artist/designer with glassblower. This idea spread throughout the Småland region, encouraging other glasshouses, especially Kosta, to make more artistic wares. Since the eighteenth century, Kosta had concentrated on blown table glass, but after 1917, under Edvin Ollers's direction, it developed innovative cutting techniques. Elis Bergh oversaw the production of nonfigural cut glass at Kosta from 1929 to 1950, when Vicke Lindstrand—an Orrefors veteran—arrived to expand the firm's repertory still further, using every technique known to Swedish glassmakers.

In recent years, Kosta has regularly employed independent Studio Glass designers such as Bertil Vallien and Ulrica Hydman-Vallien to create whimsical decorative pieces which sometimes incorporate animal motifs.

However, Swedish glass has traditionally used the brilliant refractive and reflective qualities of crystal to make the utilitarian beautiful. Sculptured objects have not been an important part of their oeuvre. Thus, animal figures are rarely made in Sweden; more often, animal motifs are engraved or painted on useful objects.

Motif from the County of Skåne 1966.
AB Orrefors Glasbruk (Sweden). Engraved lead crystal. Height: 27 cm.
Orrefors Museum, Sweden

The Dove 1937.
Edvin Ohrstrom for AB
Orrefors Glasbruk (Sweden). Full-lead crystal with
ariel technique. Diameter:
12 cm, height: 14 cm.
Courtesy AB Orrefors
Glasbruk, Sweden

Ariel c. 1925–40.
E. Ohrstrom for AB Orrefors Glasbruk (Sweden).
Vase in heavy clear glass
with blown pattern.
Height: 16 cm. The
Toledo Museum of Art,
Ohio. Gift of Mrs. Hugh
J. Smith, Jr., 1948

Vase c. 1950.
Edward Hald for AB Or-
refors Glasbruk (Sweden).
Graal glass. Height:
13 cm, diameter: 13 cm.
Cooper-Hewitt Museum,
Smithsonian Institution,
New York. Gift of Mrs.
Henry B. du Pont.

OTHER MAKERS:
EUROPE AND THE U.S.

Ring Doves 1933.
Gabriel Argy-Rousseau
(France). *Pâte de verre* vase
molded with a frieze of flying dove. Diameter:
10.5 cm. Yves Delaborde
Collection, France

Hummingbird 1930.
Aristide Colotte (France).
Crystal, carved and
etched. Height: 30 cm.
Claude Marzet Collection,
France

**"Au Soleil" Perfume Bot-
tle (Lubin)** c. 1925.
Verreries Dépinoix
(France). Molded and
painted glass. Height:
21.5 cm. Musée Interna-
tional de la Parfumerie de
Grasse, France

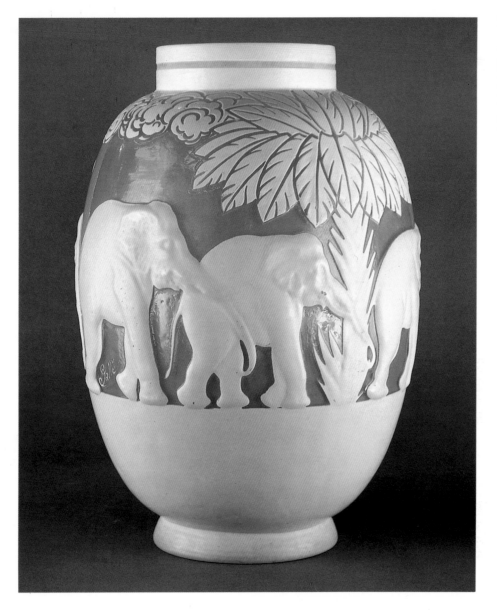

Vase with Elephant Decoration c. 1910.
Emile Gallé (France).
Blown, molded glass.
Height: 36 cm. Private
collection

Birds 1920.
Jean Sala (France). Blown
glass. Height: 11–15 cm.
Private collection

Bowl c. 1920–25.
Gabriel Argy-Rousseau
(France). *Pâte de verre.*
Height: 9.5 cm. Courtesy
Glassgallery Michael
Kovacek, Vienna

Bowl c. 20th century.
Jean Sala (France). Deep
turquoise glass with swan
decoration. Height:
13.3 cm, diameter (top):
17.8 cm. The Toledo Mu-
seum of Art, Ohio. Gift of
Mr. and Mrs. Hugh J.
Smith, Jr.

Vase with Greyhounds
c. 1928.
Marcel Goupy (France).
Enameled glass. Height:
25 cm. Georges Blache
Collection

Bottle for Cologne
France, c. 1930. Clear
glass bottle with a sala-
mander in the silvered
disk. Height: 25 cm. Mu-
sée International de la Parfumerie de Grasse, France

Vase c. 1930.
Paul d'Avesn (France).
Molded opaque white
glass. Height: 21.2 cm,
diameter (overall):
28.6 cm. Cooper-Hewitt
Museum, Smithsonian In-
stitution, New York.
Stanley Siegel Collection

Mural depicting the history of navigation 1934. Jean Dupas (France). Made for the grand salon of the liner *Normandie* (view #4 detail). Plate glass, painted on reverse; gold and silver leaf. Each panel, approximate height: 121.9 cm, width: 76.2 cm. The Metropolitan Museum of Art, New York. Gift of Dr. and Mrs. Irwin R. Berman, 1976

Vase 1926. Gabriel Argy-Rousseau (France). *Pâte de verre.* Height: 25 cm. Private collection. Courtesy Sotheby's, London

Study c. 1910–20. Almeric Walter and Henri Bergé (France). *Pâte de verre.* Width: 17 cm. Private collection. Courtesy Sotheby's, London

CH. CHAMPIGNEULLE FECIT
PARIS

Sea Trophy
France, 1974. Blue glass.
Height: 25.4 cm. Musée
International de la Par-
fumerie de Grasse, France

**Luminor or Table Orna-
ment** Late 1920s.
Frederick Carder (United
States). Crystal pigeon
with cut decorations.
Height: 15.2 cm. The
Corning Museum of Glass,
New York

**Jardinière with Illumi-
nated Glass Panel**
c. 1930.
Ely Jacques Kahn for the
Alfrèd E. Rose Gallery,
New York, executed by
Kantack & Company
(United States). Etched
glass, chromium-plated
metal, and marble.
Height: 149.9 cm. Alfred
E. Rose Gallery, New
York. Courtesy Alastair
Duncan

Fishbowl #2 1972.
Mark Peiser (United
States). Off-hand blown
glass with hot tooled deco-
ration. Height: 27.3 cm,
diameter: 26.4 cm. The
Toledo Museum of Art,
Ohio

The Big Enchilada 1975.
Richard Posner (United
States). Stained glass.
Height: 91.4 cm, width:
76.2 cm. Collection the
artist

Monkey 1938.
Alfredo Barbini (Italy).
Molded and etched green
glass. Height: 16 cm. Al-
fredo Barbini Collection,
Murano

Horse 1948.
Alfredo Barbini (Italy).
Pâte de verre sculpture.
Length: 80 cm. Private
collection

Duckling c. 1938–40.
Alfredo Barbini (Italy).
Smoked gray-green
molded glass. Height:
22.7 cm. Alfredo Barbini
Collection, Murano

Frog c. 1958.
Vera Liskova (Czechoslo-
vakia). Transparent light
green glass, cut. Height:
10.5 cm. The Corning
Museum of Glass, New
York

Elephant c. 20th century. Marianne von Allesch (United States). Figure in clear transparent blue blown glass with opaque milky blue mottling, tusks and eyes are opaque white glass. Height: 14.3 cm. The Metropolitan Museum of Art, New York. Purchase Edward C. Moore, Jr. Gift, 1929

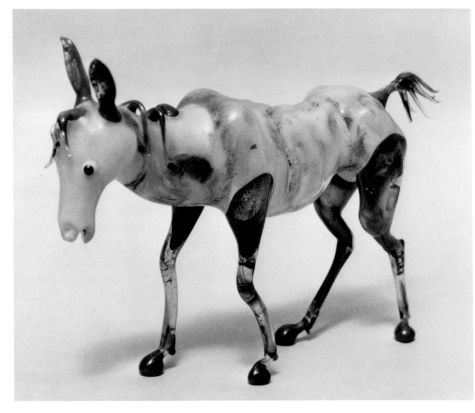

Figure of a Horse "Rosinante" c. 20th century. Marianne von Allesch (United States). Blown glass figure; mottled blue with details of brownish red. Height: 8.9 cm, width: 13.7 cm. The Metropolitan Museum of Art, New York. Purchase Edward C. Moore, Jr. Gift, 1929

Birds c. 1950.
Vistosi (Italy). Courtesy
Sotheby's, London

Bird 1974.
Wartsila Notsjoe Glass
(Finland). Red glass body
and head with blue glass
beak and blue and green
glass tail. Height:
30.8 cm. The Corning
Museum of Glass, New
York

Diana c. 1930.
Karl Hagenauer(?)
(Vienna). Colorless, lampworked tubes. Height:
27.1 cm. Courtesy Glass-
gallery Michael Kovacek,
Vienna

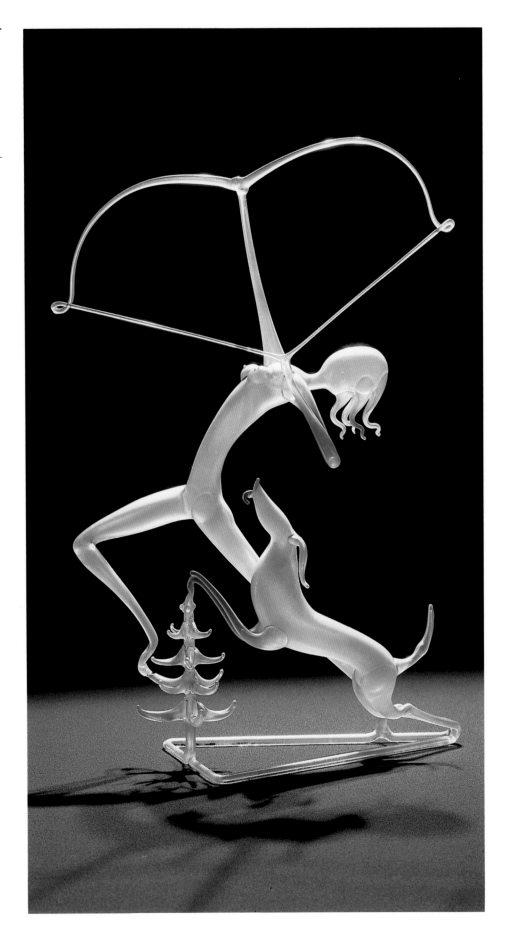

Fish Figural Bottle Adaptation
Probably Europe, c. 1930–50. Authentic bottles from New York or New Jersey, 1866–c. 1900. Design patented by W. H. Ware of Philadelphia, 1866. Blown in full-size multipiece mold for pattern and shape, neck finished, collar applied. Height: 35.6 cm. The Corning Museum of Glass, New York

Horned Animal 1965. Jaroslava Brychtova for Zeleznybrodske Glassworks (Czechoslovakia). Cast/melted glass. Height: 12.1 cm.

Fish c. 1930–40. Jean Sala (France). Bubbly green, non-lead glass; blown. Height: 16 cm. The Corning Museum of Glass, New York. Gift of Mr. Leon Andrus

GLASS AFTER 1976

Thanks to the Studio Glass Movement of the 1960s and 1970s, glass today enjoys the same status as canvas, tapestry, bronze, or marble.

The scope of the Studio Glass Movement was nowhere better documented than in a landmark exhibition titled "New Glass: A Worldwide Survey," which opened in 1979 at the Corning Museum of Glass (Corning, New York) and later embarked on a lengthy tour of many other museums in the United States, England, France, and Japan. The exhibition was organized to mark the twentieth anniversary of the Corning Museum's "Glass 1959" show, which had been comprised mainly of functional glass forms and realistic images and in which the Bauhaus values of functionalism, purity of line, and absence of decoration had dominated. In addition, most of the entries in the earlier show had been submitted by glass factories, not individual artisans.

But change had occurred in the intervening decades, and Corning wanted to assess the extent of the ever-growing Studio Movement. In 1976, the Museum issued an open invitation to artists and craftsmen in studios, academic programs, industrial institutes, and glassmaking centers throughout the world to submit slides of their best works for consideration. Of the 970 individuals who responded, 196 artists and craftsmen from 28 countries were selected for representation in the show.

The works selected by the jury were diverse and often colorful, including totally abstract pieces of glass by the Americans Harvey Littleton and Marvin Lipofsky and by the Czech Pavel Hlava. Among the minority of realistic representations were a dozen pieces depicting animals. Four of them are illustrated in this book: American artist Jamie Conover's assembled sculpture *Ricky Cow Catchers* (page 201); Swedish glass designer Ulrica Hydman-Vaillien's enameled *Blue Animal Bowl* (page 176); *Pote Machareti 345—Guanacos Relief*, a cased and sandblasted vase designed by Anselmo Gaminara and Ricardo Weisl

"Blue Animal Bowl"
1978.
Ulrica Hydman-Vallien for Kosta Boda (Sweden). Colorless and opalescent glass, blown, enameled decoration. Height: 22.5 cm, diameter (rim): 29.1 cm.
The Corning Museum of Glass, New York

for the Cristalerie San Carlos in Argentina (page 213); and a tooled glass *Elephant* by German glass designer Helmut Schäffenacker (page 202). A fifth piece, *Jaws,* by British glass engraver Ronald Pennell, illustrated on page 214, closely resembles—and is from the same *Major Egmont Brodie-Williams* series of glass designs as—one of his goblets that appeared in the show.

In general, the "New Glass" selections exhibited boundless freedom of invention. By far, most of the pieces were submitted not by glass factories but by individual artisans. Many of the submissions, in addition to being non-representational and nonutilitarian, were geometric, shaped to emphasize the fine optical properties of the glass itself. Sandblasting (in which a fine stream of emery particles is blown onto the surface of the glass, pitting it or imparting a frosty finish) was much in evidence as a decorative technique. Other forming and decorating methods seen in "New Glass" included cutting, etching, casting, slumping, molding, laminating, lampworking, and using everyday materials in innovative ways.

Besides the "New Glass" show, other important exhibitions of the late 1970s helped to showcase Studio Movement glass and to stimulate its spread internationally. They included "Modernes Glas" at Frankfurt in 1976; "Hot Glass" at London in 1976; the "Coburger Glaspreis" at Coburg, West Germany in 1977; and "Glass America" at New York in 1978. The Coburg exhibition, which included glass from seventeen countries, was especially important for documenting the emergence of an International Style of Studio Glass—based not on traditional national characteristics of glassmaking, but for the first time, on individual artistic style. Glass was now seen as a true medium of personal expression.

That trend has continued into the present. More than ever, glass has become a medium for artist as well as craftsman. Techniques seen in the "New Glass" show have persisted and are still put to good use by ever-innovative Studio Glass makers. For example, Kéké Cribbs shows remarkable ingenuity in combining materials such as wood, copper, paper, gold leaf, and shell with glass in her spirited compositions (pages 200 and 201). Cribbs is also an expert at sandblasting.

Pâte de verre is once again a favored medium for glass artists; Doug Anderson used it for *Two Plus Two Equals 40* and *Fish Fixit* (pages 203 and 200), as did Peter Yenawine for a Daum bird (page 181).

Other fresh glassworking techniques used in today's studio and factory alike include "air trapping" or sealing decorative bubbles of air within a glass object, as in Bernard Wolff's *Peacock* (page 196); mold-forming as in Lloyd

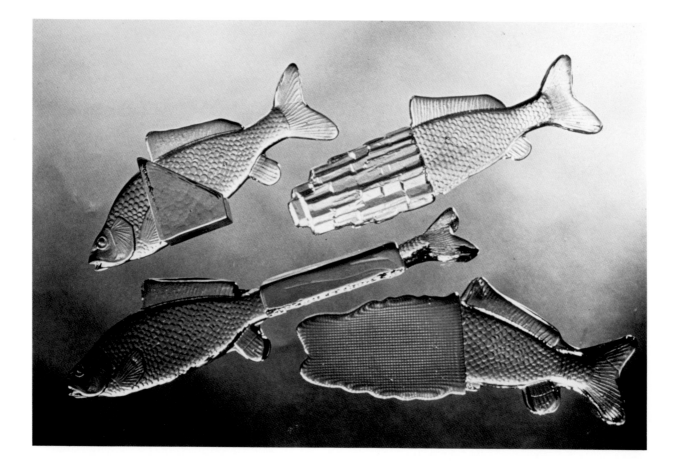

Atkins's *Cat* (page 195); and casting, exemplified by Richard Posner's *Tollpike fish*, above.

Tollpike (fish) 1981. Richard Posner (United States). Cast glass. Length: 30.5 cm, width: 15.2 cm, depth: 5.1 cm. Private Collection, Tokyo

Yenawine's collaboration with Daum illustrates another growing trend: the tendency of established American designers to spend time working in European glasshouses. For example, Dan Dailey has designed for Daum, and Marvin Lipofsky has worked at Murano for Fratelli Tosi.

As the defining characteristics of national styles become less and less apparent, glass will assume an even more important role as a medium for artistic communication. Intimately associated from the very outset with the lifestyles of human societies, glass through the ages has been like a picture book for grownups, a book in which one sees depicted all the countless efforts men have made to find new uses for a common material and new ways to enrich their homes and lives with representations of wild and domestic animals. Today, glass is a meeting ground for various trends in industry, in craft, and in art.

"Parade" 1986.
Daum, Cristallerie de
Nancy (France). Crystal
and *pâte de verre*. Height:
30 cm. Courtesy Daum,
Paris

The Dove 1983.
P. W. Yenawine for Daum,
Cristallerie de Nancy
(France). *Pâte de verre.*
Height: 28.5 cm, width:
25 cm. Courtesy Daum,
Paris

"Douce" Cat 1978.
Claude Lhoste for Daum,
Cristallerie de Nancy
(France). *Pâte de verre.*
Length: 40 cm, height:
25 cm. Courtesy Daum,
Paris

Calypso 1986.
Daum, Cristallerie de
Nancy (France). Crystal
and *pâte de verre.* Height:
22 cm. Courtesy Daum,
Paris

Persian Cat 1986.
Daum, Cristallerie de
Nancy (France). Crystal
and *pâte de verre*. Height:
14 cm. Courtesy Daum,
Paris

"Brabois" Dogs 1982.
Daum, Cristallerie de
Nancy (France). Crystal.
Length: 61 cm. Courtesy
Daum, Paris

Glass Screen with Eagle
1986.
Elisabeth Cibot (France).
Engraved glass screen
lighted with neon. Dimen-
sions: 250 × 180 cm.
Courtesy Elisabeth Cibot

King Arthur 1986.
Daum, Cristallerie de
Nancy (France). *Pâte de
verre,* cast with the lost wax
process. Height: 27.9 cm.
Courtesy Daum, Paris

Unicorn 1976.
Tauni de Lesseps for
Cristallerie de Baccarat
(France). Frosted and clear
lead crystal, gilded bronze
horn. Height: 15.2 cm.
Musée Baccarat, Paris

Eaglet 1986.
Robert Rigot for
Cristallerie de Baccarat
(France). Lead crystal.
Height: 50 cm. Courtesy
Baccarat, Paris

Cat and Dog 1986.
Robert Rigot for
Cristallerie de Baccarat
(France). Lead crystal.
Height: 52 cm. Courtesy
Baccarat, Paris

Cat and Dog

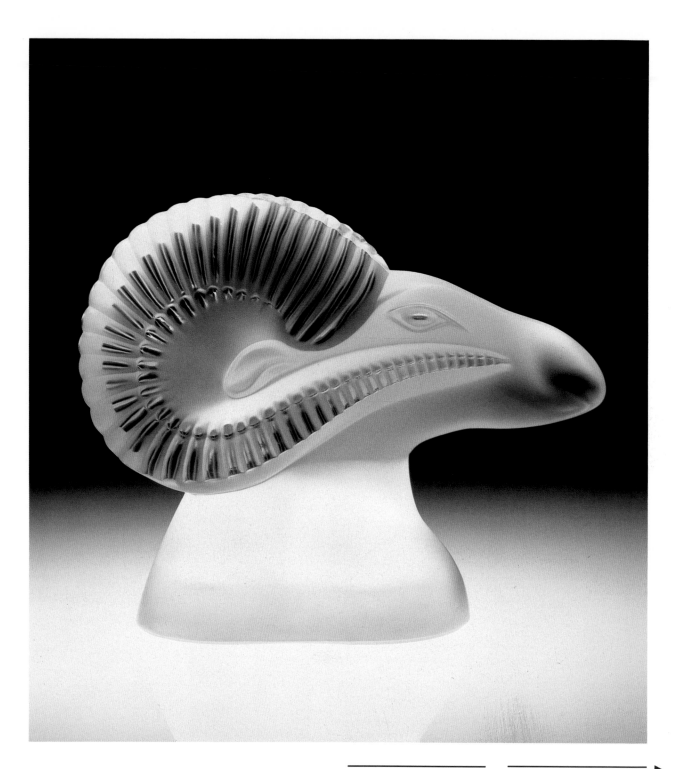

"Amon" Ram 1982.
Marie-Claude Lalique for
Cristal Lalique (France).
Frosted crystal, etched and
repolished. Length:
20 cm. Cristal Lalique,
Paris

Horned Owl 1979.
Yan Zoritchak (France).
Crystal. Height: 23.7 cm,
length: 11 cm, diameter:
6 cm. Courtesy Yan
Zoritchak

▶

"Zeila" Panther 1981.
Marie-Claude Lalique for
Cristal Lalique (France).
Satin crystal. Length:
36.5 cm. Cristal Lalique,
Paris

Vase with Owl 1982.
Marie-Claude Lalique for
Cristal Lalique (France).
Clear crystal with frosted
and engraved motif.
Height: 27.7 cm. Cristal
Lalique, Paris

Vase with Swifts 1982.
Marie-Claude Lalique for
Cristal Lalique (France).
Satin crystal. Height:
24 cm. Cristal Lalique,
Paris

"Nam" Buffalo 1983.
Marie-Claude Lalique for
Cristal Lalique (France).
Frosted crystal. Length:
36.5 cm. Cristal Lalique,
Paris

Crown of Oberon 1982. Donald Pollard (glass design) and Beni Montresor (engraving design) for Steuben Glass (United States). Blown crystal dome surmounted by a jeweled crystal-and-gold butterfly. Goldwork by Louis Feron. Height: 24.1 cm, width: 21.6 cm. Steuben Glass, New York

Bird Sphere 1978. Lloyd Atkins for Steuben Glass (United States). Blown, heavy-walled crystal sphere. Height: 20.3 cm, diameter: 24.8 cm. Steuben Glass, New York

Cicada Pendant 1978. Lloyd Atkins for Steuben Glass (United States). A solid crystal cicada, molded and fire polished, with engraved translucent wings and 18-carat gold-capped head. Pendant: length 7 cm, necklace: circumference 38.1 cm, gold 14 karat. Steuben Glass, New York

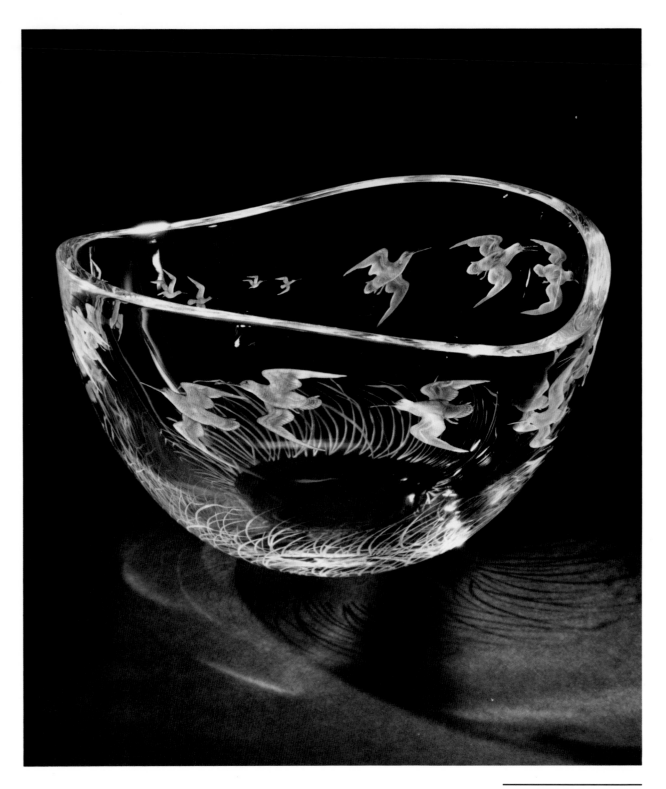

Snipe Bowl 1975.
James Houston for Steuben
Glass (United States).
Crystal. Length: 25.4 cm,
width: 21 cm, height:
15.2 cm. Steuben Glass,
New York

Herd of Elephants 1980.
Paul Schulze for Steuben
Glass (United States). A
single design composed of
three solid crystal ele-
phants, offhand and fire-
polished. Length: 22.9 cm
each, from trunk to tail.
Steuben Glass, New York

Cat (from *The Hand Coolers*
series) 1983.
Lloyd Atkins for Steuben
Glass (United States).
Solid crystal cat, molded
and fire polished. Width:
6.4 cm. Steuben Glass,
New York

Western Horses 1977. Bernard X. Wolff (glass design) and Charlotte Linnea Hallett (engraving design) for Steuben Glass (United States). Semicircular disc of solid crystal, cut and engraved. Width: 26 cm, height: 16.5 cm, depth: 5.7 cm. Steuben Glass, New York

Peacock 1986. Bernard X. Wolff for Steuben Glass (United States). Blown crystal peacock, formed offhand and cut. Width: 36.8 cm, height: 25.4 cm. Steuben Glass, New York

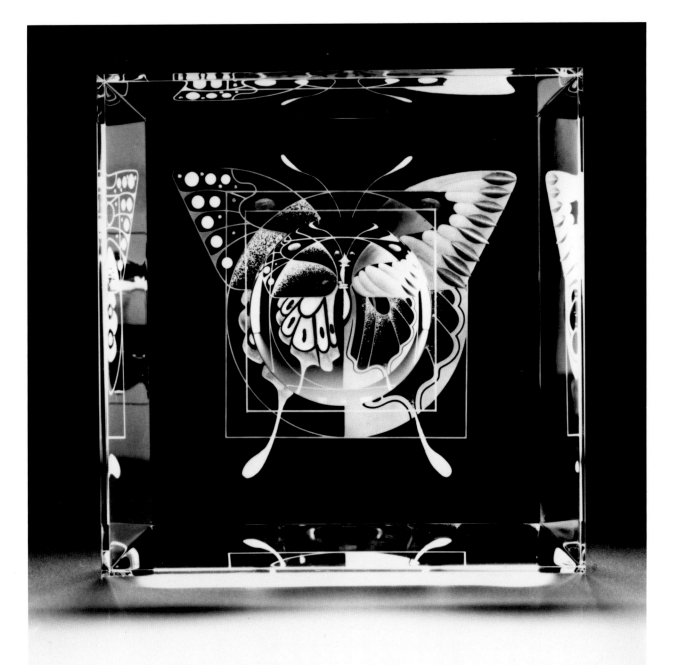

Dreaming Butterfly
1981.
Bernard X. Wolff for
Steuben Glass (United
States). Cut and polished
crystal engraving using
copper-wheel, stone-
wheel, diamond-point,
and sandblasting tech-
niques. Height and width:
15.2 cm. Steuben Glass,
New York

Earth Paradise 1978.
Claude Nicolas (France).
Engraved glass, sand-
blasted. Height: 150 cm,
width: 250 cm. Private
collection, France

Lion 1983.
Lloyd Atkins for Steuben
Glass (United States).
Solid crystal. Length:
20.3 cm, height: 9.5 cm.
Steuben Glass, New York

Girl Fish (A house where girl fishes live) 1985.
Kéké Cribbs and Dick Marquis (United States). Glass form for the body blown by Marquis, cut and polished bullseye glass for fins and background, decorated and sandblasted by Cribbs. Height: 33 cm, width: 48.3 cm. Courtesy Kéké Cribbs

Sailing to Byzantium 1986.
Kéké Cribbs and Dick Marquis (United States). White on clear sandblasted glass with gold leaf, blown by Marquis, decorated by Cribbs. Height: 73.7 cm, length: 76.2 cm. Courtesy Kéké Cribbs

Fish Fixit 1984.
Doug Anderson (United States). *Pâte de verre.* Height: 8.9 cm, width: 4.5 cm, length: 22.9 cm. Private collection

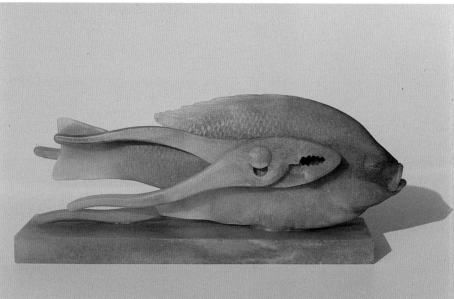

"Ricky Cow Catchers"
1977.
Jamie Conover (United States). Colored glass sculpture, slumped, lampworked, sandblasted, assembled cold; plastic turf. Height (overall): 13.8 cm, length: 21.1 cm, width: 23.3 cm. Collection the artist

Crystal Animals 1980. Bertil Vallien for Kosta Boda (Sweden). Cast in full-lead crystal, cut and polished. Height (Lion): 10 cm, length: 14 cm. Courtesy Kosta Boda, Sweden

The Elephant 1977. Helmut Schäffenacker (design) for glass artist Livio Seguso (Italy). Gray tinted glass, tooled. Height: 22.1 cm, width: 18.9 cm, depth: 7.6 cm. Museum für Kunst und Gewerbe, Hamburg

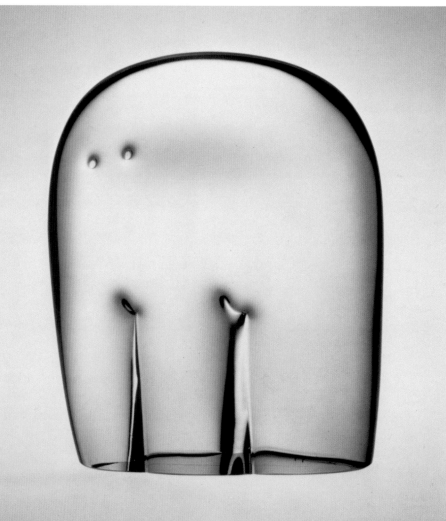

Dream of Flying 1979. Bertil Vallien for Kosta Boda (Sweden). Crystal vase, underlay technique, blown, carved, and acid-etched. Height: 18 cm, diameter 26 cm. Courtesy Kosta Boda, Sweden

Two Plus Two Equals 40 1983. Doug Anderson (United States). *Pâte de verre* (Cast Glass Sculpture). Dimensions: 11.4 × 15.2 × 17.8 cm. Courtesy Heller Gallery, New York

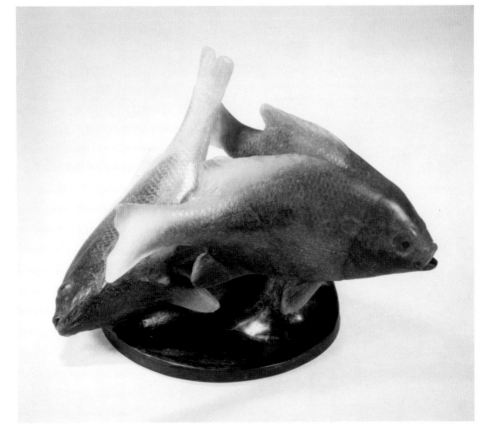

Monster #1 1985. Janet Kelman (United States). Colorless, non-lead glass with opaque lavender, amethyst, blue, tan, yellow, green, and aqua enamels; flat glass, cut, fused, sandblasted, enameled, kiln-formed over a mold. Height: 10.3 cm, length: 22.7 cm, width: 9.7 cm. The Corning Museum of Glass, New York

Shooting the Bull 1984. Dan Dailey (United States). Vitrolite glass and gold-plated metal. Length: 38.1 cm. Courtesy Heller Gallery, New York

Odyssey 1986.
Kéké Cribbs and Dick
Marquis (United States).
Glass, blown by Marquis,
decorated and sandblasted
by Cribbs. Height:
27.9 cm, width: 15.2 cm.
Private collection

"Happy Bird" 1980.
Ulrica Hydman-Vallien in
collaboration with Jan-
Erik Ritzman (Sweden).
Free blown glass, light
blue underlay in the bub-
ble. Height: 27.5 cm.
Courtesy Ulrica Hydman-
Vallien

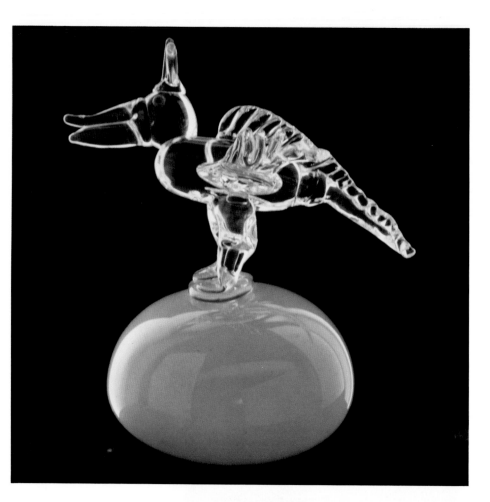

**Snake and Birds in Har-
mony** 1986.
Ulrica Hydman-Vallien for
Kosta Boda (Sweden).
Crystal (Kabale tech-
nique). Height (including
snake): 29 cm, width:
18 cm. Smålands Mu-
seum, Sweden

Peacock 1982.
Mario Ticco for VeArt
(Italy). Blown and hand-
made glass with "filigrana"
canes on black back-
ground. Claws in silver
microfusion bronze.
Height: 49.9 cm. Cour-
tesy VeArt, Italy

Chickens 1979.
Toni Zuccheri for Venini
(Italy). Translucent worked
molten glass. (Rooster)
length: 35 cm, height:
30 cm; (hen) length:
30 cm, height: 30 cm.
Courtesy Venini, Italy

The Bear 1981.
Liz Quantock (United
States). Leaded stained
glass, vitreous paints.
Height: 68.6 cm, width:
45.7 cm. Private collection, New York

Pigeon 1983.
Toni Zuccheri for Venini
(Italy). Molded glass.
Length: 25 cm. Courtesy
Venini, Italy

Pheasant 1984.
Toni Zuccheri for Venini
(Italy). Molded glass.
Length: 50 cm, height:
22 cm. Courtesy Venini,
Italy

Eskimo Dog 1981.
Mats Jonasson for Royal
Krona (Sweden). Height:
25 cm. Private collection

Animal Architecture
1985.
Frances V. Tennent (Canada). Colorless non-lead
glass with natural green
tint; cut, fused, sandblasted. Height: 21.6–
19.8 cm. The Corning
Museum of Glass, New
York

Lynx 1984.
Mats Jonasson for Royal
Krona (Sweden). Height:
27 cm. Private collection

Fairuz and the Elephant King at the Lake of the Moon 1983.
Catherine Thompson (United States). Cut, enameled, silver-stained, sandblasted, leaded. Dimensions: 69×69.1 cm. The Corning Museum of Glass, New York

**Pote Machareti 345 —
Guanacos Relief** 1977.
Anselmo Gaminara and
Ricardo Weisl (Argentina).
Colorless glass cased with
red glass, sandblasted.
Height: 23.8 cm. The
Corning Museum of Glass,
New York

Decanter "Jaws" 1979.
Ronald Pennell (England).
From a set titled: Major
Egmont Brodie-Williams
in Africa. Engraved glass.
Height: 24 cm. Courtesy
the artist

Elephant 1983.
Denji Takeuchi for Sasaki
Glass Co., Ltd. (Japan).
Cast, polished glass.
Height: 14.5 cm, width:
15.5 cm. Courtesy Sasaki
Glass Co., Ltd., Tokyo

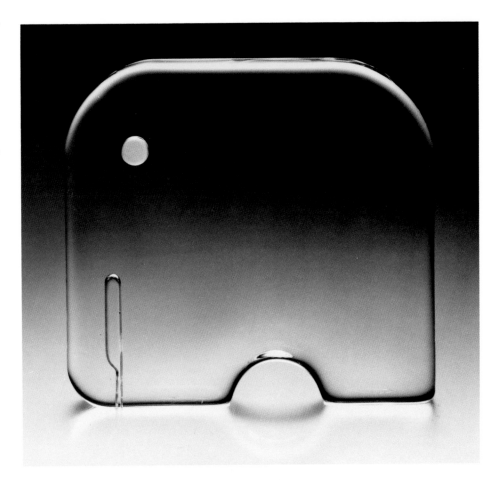

Mouse 1983.
Denji Takeuchi for Sasaki
Glass Co., Ltd. (Japan).
Cast and polished glass.
Height: 9 cm, width:
12 cm. Courtesy Sasaki
Glass Co., Ltd., Tokyo

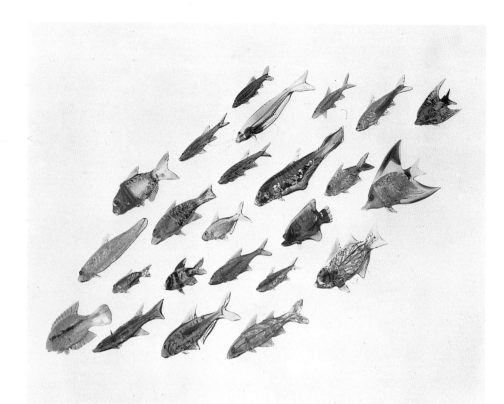

"Safari" Wall Necklace
1985.
Ronnie Wolf (United
States). Fused glass wall
necklace. Dimensions:
91.4 × 25.4 cm. Liz
Quantock Collection

INDEX

PHOTOGRAPH CREDITS

The author and publisher wish to thank the owners and custodians for permitting the reproduction of works of art in their collections. Photographs were generally supplied by the owners, with the exception of the following:

A. C. L. Brussels, 23 above, 67, 70 above right; Courtesy Janine Bloch-Dermant, Paris, 159 above, 160 below; Lee Boltin, 20 above; Bulloz, 104 above; M. and P. Chuzeville, 40 above, 44 left, 44 above right; The Corning Museum of Glass, New York, 93 above, 93 below, 202 below; D. Gaverick, 203 below; Cliff Guttridge, 214; MAAD, 71 above; Gilbert Mangin, 109 above, 114 right, 128 above left, 128 above right, 129 below; Galerie Félix Marcilhac, Paris, 110; Jacques Mayer, 74 above, 74 below; Ilona Molnar, 27 below; Mille Anni Di Arte Del Vetro a Venezia (Albrizzi Editore, 1982), 169 above, 170 above; Musée des Arts Décoratifs/photo by Laurent Sully-Jaulmes, Paris, 59, 60; Musées d'Archéologie et d'Arts Décoratifs, Liège, 112; Musées Départementaux de Seine-Maritime/photo by François Dugné, 29 below; Museo Archeologico, Locarno/photo by Dona De-Carli, 28; Museo Correr, Museo Vetrario, Murano, Archivo Fotografico, 48, 55; Dr. Parisini, Vienna, 56, 69, 161 above, 173; Photorama, 61; Jeff Ploskonka, 87; Liz Quantock, 209; Rheinisches Bildarchiv, Cologne, 26 below; Routhier, Studio Lourmel, Paris, 184, 185; Service Photographique, clichés des Musées Nationaux, Paris, 10, 15 above, 15 below, 19, 38 above, 38 below; Service Photographique de la Réunion des Musées Nationaux, Paris/photo by Christian Délu, Boulogne-Billancourt, 105, and photo by Laurent Sully-Jaulmes, Paris, 85 below, 108 left, 109 below, 131 below; Servizio Beni Culturali della Provincia automa di Trento, archivio dei documenti inventariali/photo by Elena Munerati, 47; Laurent Sully-Jaulmes, Paris (courtesy Janine Bloch-Dermant), 158 below, 160 above; Ola Terje, 206 above, 206 below; Marcel Varret, 106, 118.